Crécy

henri de wailly

Crécy
1346
Anatomy of a Battle

BLANDFORD PRESS
POOLE · NEW YORK · SYDNEY

First published in the UK 1987 by Blandford Press
Link House, West Street, Poole, Dorset BH15 1LL

World copyright © 1985 Charles-Lavauzelle, Paris
English language copyright © 1987 Blandford Press Ltd
Translated by Abdus and Joanna Sookia

Distributed in United States by
Sterling Publishing Co, Inc,
2 Park Avenue, New York, NY 10016

Distributed in Australia by
Capricorn Link (Australia) Pty Ltd
PO Box 665, Lane Cove, NSW 2066

British Library Cataloguing in Publication Data

Wailly, Henri de
  Crecy, 1346 : anatomy of a battle.
  1. Crecy (France) , Battle of, 1346
  I. Title
  944'.025   DC98.5.C8

ISBN 0 7137 1930 3

Typeset by Best-set Typesetter Limited, Hong Kong
Printed in Great Britain by
R.J.Acford Ltd., Chichester, Sussex

CONTENTS

FOREWORD

The argument concerning the dominance of cavalry over infantry — and vice versa — lasted until tanks eventually replaced the war horses of the *fervêtus* (the 'ironclads') and the robust breed of the *gros frères* ('big brothers'), the cuirassiers who had won so many victories under the Ancient Régime and the Empire. The Greek and Roman civilisations had seen the triumph of the infantry. Alexander the Great, King of Macedonia and conqueror of the Orient, had formed a magnificent cavalry to support his phalanx, but its dominance was short-lived. The Roman legion, where the horseman was reduced to the role of auxiliary, was undefeated until AD 260 when the mail-clad soldiers of King Shapur (from present-day Iran) cut Emperor Valerian's army to pieces at Edessa.

This crushing defeat caused the emperors of the Eastern Empire to reflect on the role of their cavalry. They trained a force — often victorious, but sometimes defeated — to fight the dreadful horsemen of Allah, forces that Islam sent as far as Poitiers in the eighth century. The soldier of the later Middle Ages was, in theory, a horseman. This knight, or *fervêtu,* was proud of his birth, of belonging to the Order of Chivalry and of his weapons, the lance and the sword, the pommel of which enshrined precious relics, and proud of the coat of arms that celebrated his family's glory. He scorned footsoldiers, peasants and simple provincials, whom he cut to pieces with relish during the terrible conflicts that then bloodied the fields of France, England and Germany.

At the end of the twelfth century, however, the crossbow appeared; it was a fearful weapon that pierced armour with its arrows or bolts, and was banned by the Popes. In 1302, one piece of news threw the feudal world into disarray: at Courtrai, Philippe le Bel's knights were crushed by Flemish footsoldiers; and thirteen years later, Swiss footsoldiers defeated the Archduke of Austria's feudal army at Morgarten (1315).

The Hundred Years' War broke out in 1337. The French had an overwhelming numerical superiority, but their enemies had the advantage of a refined strategy. In 1298, at the Battle of Falkirk, King Edward I of England had beaten the Scots by combining the actions of his knights with archers armed with the fearful longbow, and now the formidable English war machine was again ready for the ultimate confrontation.

Following the tactics of the earlier Saxons, the *fervêtus* of Edward III, though proud of their lineage, knew how to fight on foot and on horseback, elbow to elbow with the archers and the pikemen. King Edward and his son, the Black Prince, possessed an apparently invincible army which, in 1346, was to triumph on the day of Crécy. In this book Henri de Wailly describes the dramatic events with both expertise and insight, and in doing so enables the past to be understood and provides a lesson for the present and future: it is union which creates strength.

Emmanuel Bourassin

1 THE WAR OF SUCCESSION

The year 1346 saw the beginning of a conflict that had been smouldering for a long time. On the one hand, the English crown had never accepted the expulsion of King John of England from Normandy by Philippe Auguste; and after 140 years this English–French bone of contention still remained. On the other hand, England accepted less and less the sovereignty of the King of France over the 'English' soil of Guienne and Ponthieu. Feudal right imposed, in effect, that the sovereign of England should pay regular homage to the King of France, a requirement which England found unbearable.

In addition to all this, eighteen years previously, on the death of Charles IV, without a single male descendant, the peers of France had chosen Philippe de Valois, his cousin, as successor.

Edward III of England maintained, however, that he should have been chosen, as he was the sole direct successor through his mother to the throne of France. The French peers nevertheless cited French law: in France the 'Salic law' forbade succession to the throne through the distaff side. Edward was therefore faced with having to pay homage, for his continental fiefs, to the King of France, even though he considered that king to be a usurper.

At first, Edward III seemed to accept this. On 6 June 1329 he arrived with great pomp in France to pay homage to Philippe for Guienne and Ponthieu. Furthermore, in Amiens cathedral each appeared to welcome the other warmly, surrounded by a large court.

Edward crossed the Channel with 1,000 horses, while Philippe was surrounded by an ostentatious court, notably King Jean de Bohème, the King of Navarre and the King of Majorca who, for various complex reasons, were staying in France. There was 'such a great abundance of dukes, counts and barons it was wonderful to recall'; fifty years later the chronicler Froissart, who was nine when the battle took place, was still collecting memories of the celebration which lasted eight days.

In both London and Paris, anyone of note conversed in French. The sovereigns were cousins and many of

'The beginning of the fourteenth century can be considered as the end of the period of expansion of the medieval economy.'
Henri Pirenne, *Civilisation Occidentale,* Vol. VIII

the noble houses had fiefs or alliances on the other side of the Channel; but then hatred is often strongest within the family.

In spite of the celebrations, Edward paid only a semblance of homage to Philippe within his lands, which was surrounded by conditions and nibbled away by reservations and local restrictions: this appearance of duty therefore resolved nothing.

For three years negotiations took place and delegations were sent. Each king tried to strengthen his claim to the French throne while buying time. Neither king trusted anyone. Edward, whose father had been assassinated, feared conspiracies and, as Favier recalls, the English court had been 'a viper's nest' for twenty years. Edward had to conduct in Scotland a war that France was encouraging, while, for his part, Philippe, who was the first Valois to wear the crown, was not accepted by all the feudal lords.

Backed by the English, Brittany started to rebel. There was also the question of external interests and influences — wool from Flanders, lucrative alliances and foreign interventions, in particular from the Pope. Nothing was achieved for three years.

In March 1331, disguised as a merchant, Edward III sailed to France; in person, accompanied by only fifteen men, he met Philippe VI at Pont-Sainte-Maxence. The situation seemed about to resolve itself and, for a moment, the advent of peace could be glimpsed, but negotiations broke down again, due to trouble occurring regularly at Saintonge, Calais and Flanders.

Six more years passed. It was rumoured that Philippe was considering whether to invade England. Finally war broke out. In 1337, around All Saints Day, the Bishop of Lincoln, Henry Burgersh, brought a message to the Louvre from Edward addressed to 'Philippe de Valois, who calls himself King of France'. It was a deliberate severance of feudal ties, a renunciation of the homage at Amiens, an insult, and a declaration of war.

The first big shock took place at Sluys, near Bruges, on 24 June 1340. It was a battle fought by infantry on the decks of ships moored side by side, and a massacre followed after the French, accompanied by Genoese troops, lost the battle. The English and their Flemish allies won freedom of the seas, although Edward was seriously wounded. Three months later, on 25 September, a treaty was signed at Esplechin, near Tournai. The Hundred Years' War should therefore be regarded as a succession of bloody conflicts, sieges and raids, interrupted by short-lived treaties.

Six years later in Flanders the English began to lose

the support of their allies. Philippe saw an opportunity to capture Guienne and despatched his son, Jean, Duke of Normandy, at the head of a feudal army (comprising 60,000 men, claimed Froissart, who liked impressive numbers).

From March onwards, Jean besieged the army of *Goddons,** led by Derby at Aiguillon.

France, then the most urbanised country in Europe, was a powerful nation with a population of fifteen million. Sustained by an apparently stable feudal system, it had been successfully reclaiming land for three centuries, had built cathedrals, set off on the Crusades and was expanding into Europe. What could England with its three to four million inhabitants do against such a country?

The siege at Aiguillon dragged on. It was July, and Derby, who had informed the king of his situation, still fended off the assaults. He hoped that England would soon come to his rescue, and his hope was proved right. Edward III had gathered hundreds of ships at the ports of Weymouth, Portsmouth and Dartmouth and prepared a well-planned expedition. An English victory would be not only the result of bravery but also of meticulous organisation and good administration of resources.

According to Ferdinand Lot, to send an expeditionary force, comprising sailors as well as 16,000 men-at-arms, knights, squires, weapon-bearers, grooms, carpenters, farriers with provisions, water, tents, weapons (including probably more than 300 m^3 of arrows), 3,000 horses, chargers, palfreys, beasts of burden, forges, tools, axes, scythes, billhooks, horseshoes, nails, wagons, dishes and fodder, to anticipate all this and to order it on time required intelligence and decision on the part of Edward, and punctuality and competence on the part of clerks, workmen, sailors and the soldiers who made up the English army. The small ships, whose average weight quite probably did not exceed 100 tonnes, could not be encumbered with apprentices and novices; therefore all men were selected, trained and qualified. As Edward had strictly to limit the total strength of his expeditionary force, he chose carefully both his companions and equipment.

As Jean Favier notes, feudal recruitment and contingents brought by vassals to their king no longer existed in England. The English army was a force recruited by contract and paid for through taxation. Its fighting men were professional: noblemen of the English or Gascon knighthood, gentlemen-turned-soldiers, and Welsh or English peasants recruited to the infantry.

During the wars against the Scottish highlanders,

* *Goddons* was the nickname of the English, and was probably derived from the often used swearwords, 'God damn'.

* It can be roughly estimated that, during a battle such as Crécy, which lasted about three hours and during which 3,200 to 5,000 archers were deployed for perhaps one-sixth of the time, 150 to 230 m³ of arrows would have been used, in other words the contents of 35–55 carts of 4 m³.

Of course, all these figures are open to debate and merely serve to emphasise the logistics of the expedition. However, even if the number of carts brought by the English to the raid of 1346 is not known, it is recorded that in their raid of 1359 in France, again under the command of Edward III, '8,000 harnessed to four strong plough-horses' were brought (*Deux Siècles d'Histoire en Picardie, 1300–1498*, Lucien Lecat, Amiens, CNDP, 1982).

who were unaware and uncaring of the code and regulations of knighthood, the English learnt tactical flexibility, the art of adapting to difficult terrain and discipline. All in all, the English army was a force that France technically could not visualise. Their weapons, organisation and tactical philosophies were all different, especially the archery.

The bow itself was not a new weapon, but the concentrated way in which it was to be used by the English had a halting effect that no one in France until then had been aware of. Whereas an arrow, comparatively light and ineffectual, rarely penetrated breast-plates, it could nevertheless pierce coats of mail and protective boiled leather. Discharged in volleys in quick succession, these thousands of arrows showering down would blind the adversary, nailing him as well as his horse under him to the spot, defeating him even before he could advance. On the continent, archery such as this was a complete surprise and its reputation was soon to be known throughout Europe.

Archery had been practised in England for a long time. In the English parishes the bow was a 'compulsory hobby', and a spirit of competition raised the standard. The English archer was not just an enlisted peasant, but a proven shot; selected, paid and proud of himself. The archers thought so highly of the excellence of this weapon that, according to Louandre, they boasted they could draw blood from a weathercock with their arrows. A very good archer could shoot up to fifteen times a minute. Anyone with a speed of less than ten shots per minute would not be accepted into the army. Christopher Rothero explains that such a standard could only be reached through long training, using more and more powerful bows. The archer had to shoot quickly, accurately and rhythmically, each shaft being picked up from the ground in front of the man, taken to the bowstring, and brought back to the ear with a regular movement that involved using all the muscles of the arms, chest and back.

The good archer did not miss an enemy at a hundred metres, and a fully extended bow shot up to three hundred metres, a distance at which accuracy was unimportant. The longbow was made of wood that was strong and supple. The best was Spanish yew, the second best English yew, and the wood most commonly used was elm. According to Rothero, a bow measured between 1.6 m and 1.8 m but, Pierre Lorain tells us, it could reach 2 m. In any case, it was taller than the archer. The arrows, measuring around 90 cm, were made of all types of wood. As the halting power depended on the density of arrows, the numbers used were enormous.*

aulles que
ngeneralmet
on appelle
france. de. iii.
nations fu
rent ancienemet
composee. cest assauoir. des bestes
des celtes z des poitteuins. Les
quelles nations de dieux. de lan
gaiges z de meurs se duisoient
Les bestes sur tous les aultres
estoient les plus fors car le peu
ple de bestes estoit sans solas et
essenllez de tout aultre peuple en
uiure. en coustumes. en hantise en
uie et en meurs. dur. robuste. cest
a dire fort crueux saunaige cora
geux z hardis. ne nulz estraungiers
on peuls conuersoient auec eulx
ne ossz eulx auecq les aultres
ne communoient nullement ne
ne prendoient solas. z comment

batilloient contre lez sauons oul
tre le rin. et ce les rendoit z faisoit
estre plus crueux plus durs et
plus promptz a soustenir iiiis faus
et duroit leur retine de se mer q
entre ou rin iusques a la riuiere
de samne inclusement. cest a dire.
enclos. La seconde ptie de gaulle
estoit appellee celtes q maintenat
on dist bourgongne z duroit insqz
a le riuiere del rosne. La tierche
partie de gaulle estoit pittauia
que on dist poittiers. z smechoit
de geronde z duroit insques aux
porz despaigne. La cause de la batail
le des hericimens. Julius celsus. luca
nus et suctonius. Le second capitle.
Du tampz donques q marti
messalla et marius piso
estoient consulz de la cite de rome
z auecq eulx Julles cesar. Diteurz
duoit en la cite des hericimes vint

A GROUP OF MEN AT ARMS
*From an illustration in the 'Grandes
Chroniques de France' (1380), wearing laced
basinets and hauberks or coats of mail, with
swords and long bucklers as were worn at the
time, or little shields simply designed to ward
off blows; some of their clothing seems to have
been made of leather. Some of the footsoldiers
at the back are carrying halberds while the men
at the front, carrying swords, are horsemen on
foot. These are all professional soldiers,
trained and equipped, unlike the 'commoners'
who were simple peasants or craftsmen, called
out for a campaign.*

A GROUP OF OFFICERS
*This fourteenth-century manuscript is a good
illustration of what was worn by the marshals
and knights-banneret, who were close to the
king: coat of mail, laced bassinet, emblazoned
doublet without sleeves, brassard, cubitières,
knee-pieces. When fighting, the men carried
swords, small shields and 3-metre lances.
There was nearly a ton in weight behind the
point of the lance, with 30 to 40 kilos of
weapons, 50 kilos of war saddle with its
accoutrements and a horse weighing about 800
kilos without its protective cladding, but the
horse was practically unable to gallop.*

qil la uoulliſent leſier en nulle mein
ere car il ma nulz qi ne fuſt pauureꝫ
et ce ſeroit trop grant deſloiauteꝫ qi
ce les uoudroit requerre par ſoi fet
liꝛois ge ſcei bien qe uos dites uoir.
ozes la grãꝫ amoꝛ qe ge auoie auoꝛ
et as autres. les me ꝛoueues dire. Et
ne fuſt inconuenable choſe ne ſe auꝫ
qe le uouliſſe bien. Car trop me greua
li departimenꝫ de uos donꝫ. et des autres
ꝙ̃pignons

Ant ont parle entrauꝫ. qe li ioꝛs fu
beuꝫ a eſclaus a liſolaus. oꝛ ia auꝗꝫ
abatue la roſee. et li paleꝫ cõmenꝫ a en
plir des barons del roiaumes. Et la roie
qi ſi fu leuee. et uint la ou li rois eſtoit
et dit ſur cal. chꝛs. nos atandoꝛt leanꝫ
poꝛ aler on meſſe. Atant ſe leua li rois.
ſi eſmueueꝫ taus poꝛce qe cal qe leue
ront neſachient le deil qil oꝛ mene
Et meſire. Gauͤ comade. qe len li apoꝛt
ſes armes. et auſi fiſt lancelot. Et qント
il ſunt arme. de leur armeꝫ ſenꝫ des eſcu
er ſenꝫ des huumes. ſe uient el paleꝫ.
atrourrent loꝛ ꝙ̃pignons qil eſtoient a

apareillie poꝛ aler ale gleſſe

Vant il furent uenu au moſtier. et
il oꝛent oi le ſuͤ ſe tot iſi arme aī
il eſtoient. et il furent retoꝛne el paleꝫ
ſi ſalerent aſeoꝛ liuns de les autre. cil
qi compaignõs eſtoiēt de la queſte. Si
re fet li rois. Batemagu au roi artu.
puis qe ceſt afferes eſt enpꝛis ſi fiere
mat. qui ne puet mes eſtre leiſiez. ielo
eroie qe li ſaint fuiſſant apoꝛte ſi uie
ront le ſeiremāt auſi com cil font qi
enqſte touient entrer. Ge le uoil bien
puis qil uos pleſt fet li rois. puis qil
ne puet eſtre. autremāt.

Des fuꝛēt as clerc de leenꝫ les ſa
int apoꝛter. ſoꝛ coꝛ en feſoit le ſeue
mant de la coꝛt. et qント il furent apoꝛ
te deuāt le matre doiꝫ. ſi apella li rois
mon ſeigneur. Gauͤ. et lioit uos eſmeu
uiſtes pmiremāt ceſte queſte. Veneꝫ
auant et ſi fereꝫ le ſeiremāt qe cil
touoient fere. qi en ceſte queſte uoꝛ

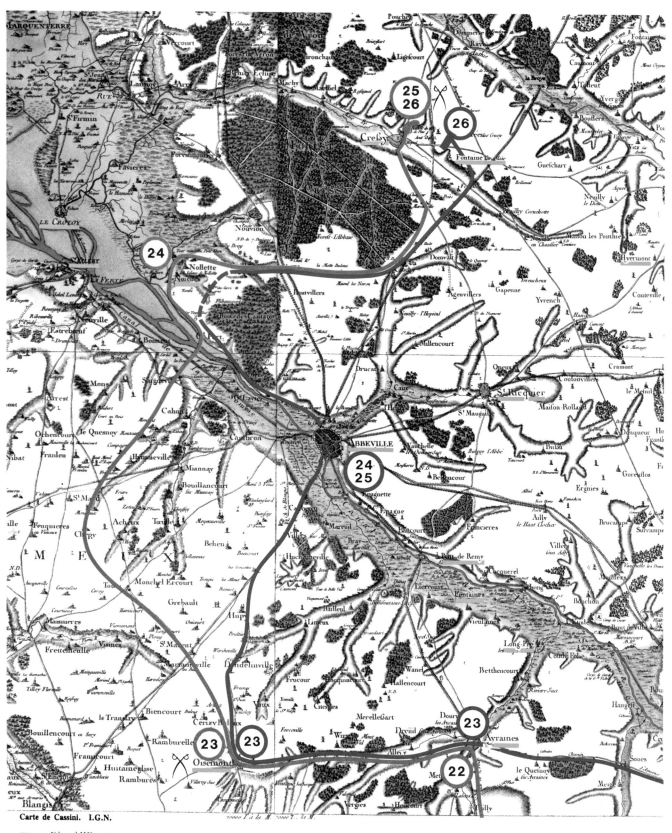

Carte de Cassini. I.G.N.

Edward III's army
Philippe VI's army
The names underlined are mentioned in the Chronicle

16

The archer carried two bundles of 24 arrows (little more than three minutes of shooting) and in battle he was supplied with arrows by weapon-bearers. He carried a sword at his side and if the battle came close he fought like a simple footsoldier. An archer did not relish this thought, for if he was taken prisoner and recognised as an archer, his thumb, index and middle finger would be cut off.

After the English archers had shot their arrows, there came the turn of the pikemen. Jean Michelet said of these men, 'they knew no French, no English and no chivalry'. There was, in fact, no language in which to plead or bargain with these 'rough, half-savage fellows from Wales, Ireland or Cornwall'. Pikemen were insensitive to both pleas and threats, and even to promises of wealth made by unhorsed knights; they were interested only in finishing their bloody task.

After the fray, the pikemen's job was to finish off what had been started and to kill the wounded. For this purpose, they used a long cutlass securely fixed to the end of a pike. They went from body to body, looking for a chink in the armour, in order to slaughter the victims. It was their profession. They did not appear to carry out this quiet massacre with any passion — on the contrary, the pikemen worked under orders and used their own judgement as necessary. Such butchery was costly, however; the more dead the less the ransom. Consequently, knights were sometimes spared.

It is generally thought that during battle they remained amongst the archers on the front line, one knee on the ground, with their pike forward to stop the enemy's cavalry.

Behind the footsoldiers, the English cavalry remained in reserve. It was an easily-manoeuvrable rather than powerful force, as opposed to the European cavalry which consisted only of nobles. Saurel recalls that a great number of rich self-equipped gentlemen were always to be found. This English army, which had trained in the war against Scotland, and was selected and governed by strict discipline, constituted a quasi-professional military force. It was no longer, as in France, a gathering of brave barons, ready to obey only if they wished to, escorted by a crowd of footsoldiers recruited the day before from their villages and fields. These English soliders did not seek to shine by individual feats, but to win while sustaining as few casualties as possible. They were soldiers and not an armed crowd.

Edward had gathered his army by the beginning of July. He set sail for Bordeaux, although it would appear that the prospect of the long crossing had left

'In the spring of 1336 England feared a French invasion: in order to prevent the Valois from becoming involved in the Scottish affair, it was best to attack him on the continent.'
Jean Favier, *La Guerre de Cent Ans*.

A map by Cassini (1750). The hills are quite clear on this map, as are the woods and forests, in particular the 'Bois de Cantâtre' which was cleared in the middle of the nineteenth century. The winding path followed by the English forces is explained by the fact that they had to avoid driving their baggage train through marshes, and also avoid covering their archers by the forest trees. The patrols sent out by Warwick at Crotoy and Rue, together with the reports made after reconnaissance towards Abbeville and Saint-Riquier on 24 August, convinced King Edward that he should change his route towards the east. The English army camped at Noyelles for the night of 24 to 25 August. The place names underlined in red are those mentioned by Froissart.

him hesitant. It was his duty and it was in his interests to rescue Derby, but he was also consigning the power of all his kingdom to the sea in one action.

On Wednesday 12 July the weather was fine on the Channel, with a westerly wind blowing. Off Saint-Vaast-la-Hougue, hundreds of sailing ships appeared on the horizon, approached land, reached the deserted beach and then ran aground. An enormous crowd of men disembarked: it was Edward III's army.

The wind had been against the fleet since it left England, and soon it grew in strength. Now the ships were no longer moving. At sea, Edward finally took the advice of one of his counsellors, Geoffroy d'Harcourt, a Norman knight banished from France, who had advised Edward before sailing to disembark in Normandy rather than undertake a long crossing.

'You will reach France on a single tide. No one in Normandy will oppose us. The country is rich. You'll march to Paris. You could also put an end to the siege at Aiguillon!'

Edward still chose Bordeaux as his target, but realising that they were not moving at sea Geoffroy d'Harcourt reiterated, 'You see, God wants us to go to Normandy!' Edward III remained undecided.

Two marshals of the king who were on board, the Earls of Arundel and Warwick, when consulted, sided with Geoffroy d'Harcourt, which decided the king. So it seems that it was at sea that Edward chose his definite target, with no forward planning. This element of surprise was to work in his favour. He had the initiative of the day, the place and no one in front of him.

Edward was thirty-four years old and a proven campaigner. He had been king for nineteen years and he knew how to command his men. Edward was wise, grave, deliberate and obeyed. He wore his hair long down his back, and his face was serious. Having been subjected to the rule of his mother (whom he eventually imprisoned) for a long time this grandson of the French king Philippe Auguste had spent part of his youth in France at Ponthieu, his mother's fief. He was often chivalrous, following the custom of the time, as well as experienced, cunning, far-sighted, cruel and competent. The danger he was in, against unknown adversaries, was great, but he had relatively unlimited resources.

His landing was a direct and intentional threat to the French throne. Philippe VI had no alternative but to use all available resources to defend himself.

2 THE RAID

The Normans believed war to be something belonging to the past and had lost the habit of guarding their defences. City walls were in a poor state, gates insecure, sentries slack, and city boundaries often unable to contain the sprawling outskirts. Favier wrote that Edward had landed in a trusting country without defences. He took full advantage of this.

At first Edward took his time. If one believes Christopher Rothero, it took six days to disembark, get ready, organise the 'battles', in other words the units or 'battalions', and set off.

The vanguard marched under the orders of the fifteen-year-old Edward, Prince of Wales, the middle section under the king's orders and the rearguard under those of the Earl of Northampton. The fleet followed the coastline. Each evening the marshals, who often marched on the extreme flanks under Geoffroy d'Harcourt and the Earl of Warwick, reunited with the king's billet.

The English brought with them terror, pillage, rape, murder and arson-horrors that were widespread and soon common practice. Barfleur surrendered immediately to avoid a massacre (the castle alone held out) and the English began to load their ships with booty: cloth, furniture, clothes, jewels and even rich noblemen for future ransom money.

At Cherbourg it began again, although once again the castle held out. The English army then marched south, leaving a trail of smoke. Valogne, Sainte-Mère-Eglise and Montebourg were all completely ransacked and burnt, as were numerous villages and hamlets. According to Froissart, a chronicler who is considered pro-English, the English also seized an astonishing quantity of loot.

Carentan made a show of resistance until the English deployed their forces to hem in the town. The show of strength was so frightening that it was sufficient for the town to surrender, apart from the castle. The English continued their siege until the castle conceded, and jewels, furniture and noblemen joined the Barfleur and Valogne booty already on the vessels.

The English army set off again. Geoffroy d'Harcourt, on his home ground, scoured the countryside either in front or on the flanks. After 15 or 20 kilometres, he sent out a squadron of 500 armoured soldiers and mounted archers. He terrorised a land where he found 'the barns full of corn, houses filled

'In the Quettehou church, built a century earlier, overlooking Saint-Vaast, Edward III knighted his son, the Prince of Wales, William of Montaigu, Roger of Mortimer, Guillaume de Roos and many others'. From the *Cambridge Chronicle*.

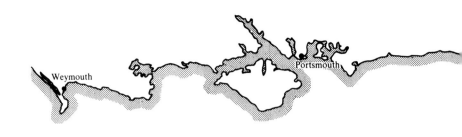

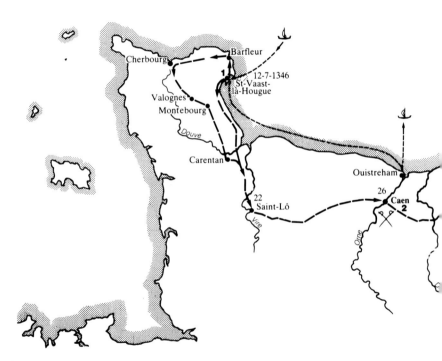

ITINERARY OF EDWARD III, IN
FRANCE IN 1346

1. Saint-Vaast-la-Hougue. 12 July 1346.
Edward III disembarks by surprise with about
12,000 men.

2. Caen. After pillaging the region of
Cotentin, the English accepted battle and took
Caen, where a terrible massacre took place.
The English fleet returned to England with a
considerable amount of booty.

3. Wanting to join his Flemish allies, Edward
III approached the city of Rouen, which
refused to fight or to allow him to pass. The
English withdrew.

with all sorts of riches, the fattest oxen and cows, ewes, sheep and pigs'. The English, who met no resistance, were amazed at all the riches they managed to accumulate.

In Paris, everything was already known — Cotentin, Edward, the archers, Harcourt, the plundering — all was being reported. Philippe de Valois was warned that unless action was quickly taken Caen would be captured. Being Normandy's second town after Rouen, Caen was an important fortress, the biggest between the English and Paris.

Philippe VI was 53 years old, which was old for that era, but this beardless man with short hair still looked

4. Poissy. Edward settled here, burned St Germain, St Cloud and Boulogne and then built a bridge over the Seine which he crossed on 15 August.

5. After burning Cormeille, Chars and Gisors, Edward fought the French at St Just, near to Beauvais, and continued forced marches towards the North.

6. Airaines. The English tried in vain to cross the Somme, which the French held throughout its length. They burned Poix, Oisemont, Aumale and Sénarpont.

7. At dawn on 24 August, Edward III managed at last to cross the Somme at the ford of Blanquetaque which no longer exists today.

8. Pursuing the English, Philippe VI, King of France, crossed the Somme at Abbeville in his turn. He remained there for a whole day.

9. In camp at Crécy, fed and rested, the English were waiting for the French, who came up in great numbers but in disorder. The battle started during the evening of 26 August.

young. It was said of him, 'he has the impetuosity of youth'. In fact, he was an impulsive man who mistrusted everything, kept his thoughts to himself, worried too much, then abruptly made up his mind. It was also said of him that, far from being intelligent, he was even ignorant, and did not know how to formulate a plan or demand an exact execution of a decision. All in all he was, in fact, a feudal king, courageous, preferring battle to strategy, distrustful rather than prudent, indecisive and secretive rather than deliberate.

Philippe had been surprised; he was expecting the English in Flanders or Guienne, and certainly not in Normandy. Nevertheless, he reacted quickly, immediately dictated and despatched messages to his troops, vassals, commoners and mercenaries, and to his allies to join him and prepare themselves for battle. He especially requested his son, Jean de Guienne, to return with his army.★ Although he was not aware of it, in only ten days Edward III had achieved his main goal of the war; to raise the siege of Aiguillon.

To ward off the immediate threat on Caen, Philippe ordered the Counts of Eu and Ghines, high constables, as well as the Count of Tancarville, to hold and block the English on the Orne. They left Paris straight away and reached Rouen, where they stayed for four days to reassemble the troops, and where it was learnt that Saint-Lô had fallen on the 22nd; it was, therefore, necessary to act quickly. The French rushed to Caen with arms and provisions. The English approached, continuing their leisurely foray: setting off in the early morning, occasionally pillaging, and stopping before midday to avoid the hottest hours. The soldiers were now so burdened with loot that they had almost stopped pillaging, not knowing what to do with the booty. Geoffroy d'Harcourt, who originated from Saint-Sauveur-le-Vicomte and knew the region well, had said, 'We will be entering one of the richest and most lavish countries in the world. We will do all that we wish because the Normans are simple people, who do not know anything of war.'

In its military wanderings, however, the English army had remained ordered. Caen had been reached and they were going to fight. Edward made preparations. The fleet, which was still following the coastline, arrived that evening at Ouistreham, where it dropped anchor, fully laden with loot.

In Caen on the 25th of July everyone was making merry and drinking, as was the custom before battle. It was known that the English had struck camp two leagues from the town that evening. The Normans were confident. The next day they would leave the

★ According to Ferdinand Lot, Philippe VI's order reached Jean de Normandie on 20th August, and he carried it out immediately. However, Jean would enter Paris on 1st September, five days after the Battle of Crécy. According to Favier, Jean was at Limousin when he learnt of the disaster, and harshly criticised his father's command. The English, on his heels, were to pillage Saintonge and take Poitiers where the adversaries would meet again in ten years.

EDWARD III IN HIS SHIP

A picture of the battle of Kadzand taken from the Breslau manuscript, Berlin. Although the ships were entirely handled by soldiers, they were not yet true warships; merchant ships were used for purposes of war before guns were invented. The first cannon shot at sea was fired in 1338 by an English ship, the Christophe de la Tour. *In this case all the soldiers are wearing armour — there was nothing to save any man who fell overboard. Note the size of the English bows, longer than a man. Also note the ships with the rudder in the centre line* à la navarraise, *which had just been invented.*

There were fore and stern castles on which the crossbowmen and the archers stood at their combat stations. There was a hold under the deck; the ports in the forecastle show that there was a lower deck. A single square sail hangs from a single mast on which is mounted a crow's nest. Only the Royal ship flies the English flag. If the illustration can be believed,

Edward III is in complete armour and is hiding his beard behind his gorgeret. The English disembarked in July 1346 at Saint-Vaast-la-Hougue from hundreds of ships like these.

ramparts and annihilate the English in a well-conducted battle. This would avoid a long siege.

On the morning of the 26th, the Normans left the town and discovered the *Goddons* — who were most impressive. There were banners at the fore, and streamers and pennants fluttered in the wind. The English rode on horseback or marched tightly ranked, grouped in units, evenly and with precision. They halted when ordered, and manoeuvred without fuss. The French, intimidated by this ordered deployment, watched while the English archers took up their position. They shot when commanded, and the arrows flew simultaneously, showering down. There was utter amazement and, wounded in great numbers even before reaching the enemy, the Normans panicked. Some fell but many retreated. The English forces were terrifying and the defenders of Caen, overtaken by panic, soon fled in total disorder. The English followed over the bridges and through the gate, and those Normans who were not able to reach the castle before the gates were shut were lost. Everyone found was killed on the spot, whether it was in the streets, houses or gardens. Froissart records that from the castle were seen 'such horrible acts of cruelty on the streets that it was hideous...to behold'.

Some people in the town tried to defend themselves. They threw stones from the roofs at the English, who lost about 500 men. The furious Edward ordered the execution of every living thing and the burning of the town: nothing was to be spared.

Geoffroy d'Harcourt, 'who liked the town of Caen', pleaded for it with Edward; and his arguments, if one is to believe Froissart, shed some light on the English intentions.

'The town is yours,' said Geoffroy d'Harcourt. 'If you push the survivors too far they will fight and you will lose more useful men: you will have many more encounters before you reach Calais.'

Edward, who wanted to return to England without needing to enter Paris, gave in to Geoffroy's reasoning. He would stop the killings. On 26th July Caen fell into Edward's hands and its castle surrendered.* The Orne was crossed.

The route to Paris was open to the English even though they had no intention of using it. It was a triumph. Lavisse advises us that, apart from London, at this time there were no towns as big as Caen in England. The English acquired an enormous booty as they were no longer killing. For four days the English 'fetched, carried and collected all good things, materials, fabrics, beds, furniture', from houses, castles, depots and shops. Lavisse specifies that they took

* The Count of Eu, who was unable to pay his ransom, was freed four years later and was subsequently beheaded for treason by King Jean le Bon.

40,000 lengths of material. All was transported on carts to Ouistreham and loaded on ships to be taken to England.

The fleet set sail with 200 men, 400 archers and 500 prisoners. On 29th July, Edward left Caen. From that moment on, he was out of touch with England.

He went to Louviers, which was unfortified. The English looted selectively; they no longer wanted to be burdened with large pieces of furniture, as they now had to carry their booty themselves. They took jewels, leaving the jewel cases, and resold what they had just taken from the owners back to them at inflated prices.

(Coll. Gaignières, Paris.)

BUST OF PHILIPPE VI DE VALOIS

King of France, 'taken from a painting on wood. The portrait is in fairly good taste and appears to have been painted in his time because the type of bonnet was then in use.' This observation was written in the eighteenth century and accompanies this engraving which was made between 1695 and 1715, after the original which has disappeared.

'They sold 100 florins for the value of 1,000 and thus made a lot of money.'

Louviers seems to have got off lightly: but unfortunately the English rearguard set fire to it on their way out. Moreover, in the county of Evreux, everything was burnt except the fortresses.

Edward was warned that Philippe had raised an army and could attack him at any time. He realised he could not linger any more, but had to cross the Seine rapidly; so he increased the pace. He tried to cross at Rouen, which held, and retreated: the town refused the orderly battle that Edward proposed. The bridge at Pont-de-l'Arche was destroyed. Edward continued south, burning everything he could whilst avoiding the castles. At Mantes, at Meulan — everywhere the bridges had been destroyed. Only the remains were left at Poissy. Edward summoned his carpenters, consulted them and instructed them to re-establish the route. They started on construction that lasted five days.

Meanwhile, the plunderers scoured the country, burning and terrorising Saint-German-en-Laye, Saint-Cloud and Boulogne. They even went as far as the outskirts of Paris, where people were starting to panic. The old twelfth-century city walls, barely maintained, were undefendable. In some areas of the city they had been buried amongst the houses. They could not even be seen between the Louvre and the Porte Saint-Denis. Elsewhere only chains restricted access; Paris could justifiably fear the fate of Caen.

Armed men arrived every day. According to Favier, the French king felt himself betrayed by Olivier de Clisson in Brittany and Geoffroy d'Harcourt in Normandy. Was he also being betrayed by others?

Whilst Edward advanced up the left bank of the Seine, Philippe in his restlessness left Paris for Rouen before returning doleful and worried to the Louvre. According to Lavisse, Philippe at last decided to request battle. He sent a herald to Edward, who replied vaguely that he wished to move away from Paris for Montfort-l'Amaury.

The 15th of August was the feast of Notre-Dame. With his now considerable cavalry, Philippe left for Saint-Denis, telling the worried Parisians that he was going into battle.

Edward, on the other hand, paraded in the Abbey of Notre-Dame-de-Poissy. He held solemn court, dressed in a sleeveless tunic over a scarlet robe lined with ermine, thus maintaining his 'royal state in all things, receiving as well or even better than he would do in England'. After all, was he not, as he maintained, the king of France itself?

3 THE CHASE

The military route march was over. Edward's court put aside its displays: the bridge at Poissy was repaired. Now it was a question of proceeding quickly. At Saint-Denis Philippe had raised the war standard and his forces increased in numbers every day; and on the 15th of August the English had crossed the Seine, jostling 3,000 French footsoldiers, entered Vexin and taken the direction of Flanders.

Philippe gave pursuit, and a long chase began. Edward's army which, up until then, had covered an average of 10 kilometres a day, more than doubled its pace until the army managed about 23 kilometres a day, an incredible distance.

The roads of the time (and the only 'roads' to speak of were the bumpy remains of the rare Roman roads, which had been occasionally cobbled and restored earlier by Queen Brunhilda) were no more than narrow overgrown paths. The ruts were deep and the directions were imprecise. It was a perilous undertaking for Edward to force-march thousands of men with horses, wagons and quite probably herds of cattle in uncertain conditions across an unknown territory which would have been far more heavily wooded than today, deserted by all its inhabitants, without any directions apart from those of the guides. Disorder was the main threat to the units. Both wounded and stragglers would be killed by hiding peasants, whilst the bulk of the army marched on. Apart from this immediate danger, there was now Philippe and his knights.

Edward protected himself by spreading panic in the surrounding countryside. His passage was marked by trails of smoke — for the houses of the period were thatched. The outskirts of Pontoise, of Cormeille-en-Vexin, of Chars and Gisors were razed to the ground. Vexin was laid to waste.

Far from the main body of the army Geoffroy d'Harcourt, the Earl of Warwick and Renauld of Cobham sent out detachments, and Beaumont-sur-Oise and Gournay-en-Braye were burnt. The vanguard approached Beauvais. In sight of Saint-Just, 4,000 French footsoldiers from Amiens and Beauvais attempted to block the way. They fought 'valiantly enough' but lost, and many were killed. Prisoners numbering 200 were taken, the rest scattered. The road to the north remained open. The next day the bulk of the English army passed near Beauvais, burnt the

'The maintenance of the roads was left to their users. In France, royalty, even in the surroundings of the capital, left the upkeep to those who used them. In winter it was more or less impossible to travel.'
Henri Pirenne, *Civilisation Occidentale,* **Vol. VIII.**

Collection Rivet, 16, rue J. Brûlé

This photograph was taken at the end of the nineteenth century at St Valéry-sur-Somme and depicts one of the last examples of traditional rural houses built of cob, or clay, on stone foundations and covered with thatch, as they existed in the fourteenth century. We see that even the gables were covered with straw and that the wall frames, doors and roof were all inflammable. Not many torches would be needed to fire a whole village. It appears that what Froissart called a hôtel *was a house built entirely of stone.*

outskirts and destroyed the Abbey of Saint-Lucien. That evening it camped at Grandvilliers. Dargies was captured on the following day, and its castle was burnt, as was everything as far as Poix, whose two undefended fortresses were taken.

The people of Poix immediately offered a ransom to avoid being burnt. The next day, as they were receiving payment, the bulk of the English having moved away, the people of Picardy changed their minds, and challenged and attacked those English who had remained to receive their due. The army (only a league away) was alerted; it stopped, and men were sent back. A massacre took place; the town and castles were razed to the ground, and no one survived. The army continued on its way to Airaines, still destroying 'to the left and to the right'.

Airaines, like Poix, was basically a fortified town that was also protected by two fortresses, but the garrison (which housed only 180 men) withdrew to Pont-Rémy at the approach of the English. Edward took the town without a struggle and set up camp. Since Poissy, the footsoldiers had covered 140 kilometres in six days and the army needed time to rest.

'The English king forbade on pain of hanging the burning of this place: his exhausted troops needed rest and his intention was to remain protected by these two fortresses for two or three days.'

The English rested, slaughtered cattle, lit ovens and made bread. Edward no longer knew which direction to take. Were the bridges of the Somme still free? He sent Warwick and d'Harcourt with 1,000 armed men and 2,000 mounted archers to reconnoitre. These forces came up against defences held by the French. Bridges had been burnt at Picquigny, Longpré and Fontaine, and at Long and Pont-Rémy were impossible to cross. The French had secured each crossing. The situation became grave. Edward learnt that Philippe's enormous army was approaching: it was now at Amiens, a day's march away.

'Much reflecting', the English king summoned his council. Henceforward time was against him. There remained only limited options: either to take the bridges of Abbeville or risk a ford that was said to exist somewhere between Abbeville and the sea. Edward may well have considered taking Saint-Valéry-sur-Somme, which, being both a port and a fortress, could shelter the English.

It was from that exact place, nearly three centuries earlier, that William of Normandy had left to conquer England. The worst of the options would be to wait there. Sadly for the sake of the soldiers' rest, the army had to proceed, and approach a crossing, even if they did not know which to use. 'Better to wait after the crossing than have the crossing wait for us,' it was being said amongst Edward's followers; therefore it was decided that they would leave Airaines very early the next day.

On the morning of 23rd August, the *Goddons* left, starting fires and using divertionary raids to disconcert the following army. Edward, accompanied by only 200 horses, went to reconnoitre Abbeville where the bridges were hidden by powerful ramparts. These were the last bridges before the Channel. Louandre relates that Edward, whose party burnt the Priory of Mareuil on their way, went in person to Caubert Hill, where the view extends over the whole valley and Abbeville, which it dominates from a height of about 70 metres. That old military site with which history had not yet finished was already defended by a Celtic citadel, known as 'Caesar's camp'. Edward surveyed the road to Abbeville, a city he knew well, for he had lived there twenty years earlier with his mother, Isabella, when he was thirteen, from 1312 to 1315. Abbeville was the capital of Ponthieu, his mother's former fief.

Would Abbeville welcome him? Edward doubted it. Abbeville had been a freetown for 150 years and was

Caesar's Camp of Mareuil-Caubert: 'The fortified hill that dominates the Somme north of Abbeville had been occupied by the military during many troubled periods of history. Thus, at the end of May in 1940, a German bridgehead fought off violent counter-attacks led by Charles de Gaulle.'
Roger Agache, *Détection aérienne*, Fig. 282.

proud of its independence. It had never ceased to show its dislike in submitting to the English presence. Only the previous year, the furious people of Abbeville, ruined by the English taxes, had forced Edward's men to lock themselves in the castle.

By observing his town, Edward soon knew what to expect: the local troops who had located this English unit at Caubert appeared from the city walls. Edward and his knights retreated. Would Edward abandon this last chance, the last bridge that separated him from his fief? He ordered Warwick and d'Harcourt to go up to the fortress walls with their 3,000 knights.

Encouraged by their mayor, Colart-le-Ver, the people of Abbeville, like those of Caen, left their fortifications supported by horsemen and 2,000 men on foot raised from other freetowns. The question was now whether the English longbow would lose its precision when fired from horseback and whether the volley fire would be sufficient. Whatever the answer, the people of Abbeville countered, attacked and 'killed 500 English and took quite a number prisoner'. The English retreated.

Edward, realising that surprise attack was impossible, changed direction towards Oisemont, burning and ravaging the country, 'such that the sparks flew as far as Abbeville'. Sparks in the sky above a town which contained thatched wooden houses was a serious hazard not to be forgotten.

All the inhabitants of Vimeu had moved to Oisemont. When they saw the English approaching, they left the unfortified town and advanced under the orders of Sire de Boubers. They fought, losing many men, and then retreated. The English captain, John Chandos, routed them and took Boubers prisoner, 'with many other fighters' of distinction.

The English, who had won the battle but lost some time, entered Oisemont, and Edward took lodgings there★ whilst waiting for his marshals.

Geoffroy d'Harcourt had failed at Saint-Valéry-sur-Somme, which the Counts of Saint-Pol and Hui were defending. Chandos had gone to burn Aumale and Senarpont as this was on his route. That evening they learnt that Philippe's army was already at Airaines. The distance between the two forces was now only 20 kilometres. Edward found himself in a critical situation; his only means of escape was the ford between Abbeville and the sea. If the English did not locate this, it would mean their being surrounded against the coast, and a massacre would ensue; Philippe would never forgive six weeks of pillaging and arson, nor the threat to his throne and the public humiliation.

Edward, who had lived in 'English' Ponthieu, knew

★ Froissart says that he stayed at the *Grand Hôpital*. This had nothing to do with the present Oisemont hospital which was then a leper-hospital. Francois d'Anzel confirms that *Grand Hôpital* meant the old Commanderie de Malte (charitable knights), which was situated near the church and has now disappeared. The old church itself collapsed in ruins less than twenty years ago. A local tradition states that the old stone cross, near the town, marks the grave of the French victims of the combat.

of the ford. He may well have seen it as a boy. The ford was maintained as a bridge and any peasant from the area could lead travellers to it. Would young Edward, the English heir, have taken this sodden route, this cattle track, rather than the bridges of Abbeville if he had been south of the river, in 'French' Vimeu? It is unlikely.

Froissart, being pro-English, gives numerous details of what happened that evening at Oisemont. Edward asked many knights, natives of Picardy taken prisoner that day, if they could show him the way to this all-important ford. Even though he promised them great courteousness, each, 'for his honour', apologised, saying he did not know it.

Edward then summoned those of lesser rank, footsoldiers who were also prisoners, and asked them the same question, promising a hundred gold nobles and a horse (a fortune), as well as the freedom of five or six prisoners, in return for an answer.

One of the men, Gobin Agache, was from Vimeu and lived at Mons, a nearby village. Like everyone there he knew the ford, as it was less than a league from his house. He could not understand what was so special about the ford. Yet such a fortune was being offered to him, and he was so sure he would never be freed for ransom, that he was soon tempted.

Gobin talked, in the Picard dialect, of course, which was then translated for the king. How could this frightened cowherd, surrounded by watchful knights, have appreciated the unparalleled importance of such an apparently trivial piece of information?

'Twelve men abreast could easily cross it, twice between night and day with the water reaching only up to their knees,' Gobin insisted. 'When the tide comes in, the river rises so high that no one could cross it, but when the tide is low the Somme is so shallow at this spot that it is easily crossed on foot as well as on horseback.'

'The bed of the ford that I refer to, your royal Highness, consists of white marl, hard and strong, where carts can pass with complete safety. That is why the crossing is called *Blanquetaque*!'

So there it was — the information Edward needed.

Edward issued orders to raise camp at midnight. There would be three trumpet calls. On the first call, the army would get up and arm itself. On the second call, the army would load up, and everyone would take up position in his unit. On the third call, they would set off. The army dined, then briefly slept. At midnight the trumpet was sounded. Before daybreak, led by Gobin, the English were on their way: knights, archers, pikemen, beasts of burden and carts.

A noble d'or. This photo was kindly supplied by M. Emile Bourgey, an expert appointed by the court of appeal. These coins were 'struck' by the kings of England after Edward III. On one side is the bust of the king wearing the shield of England above his ship, and on the other side a Gothic cross decorated by lilies. The wording is in Latin, for the king was king both of England and of France. A hundred golden nobles such as this, a horse and liberty for five or six other men was sufficient to decide a 'traitor'. Some dispute this fact saying that Edward was aware of the existence of the Blanquetaque ford, which was probable. Gobin Agache may have shown the way to the track that led to the ford. Lot said that Agache was not a traitor because he was Edward's vassal. But Mons is in Vimeu — in 'France'. Popular traditions confirm Froissart's story because, in the language of Picardy, the inhabitants of Mons are called ché trait'ed Mons ('those traitors of Mons').

32

In the dark, having barely slept, the English marched in tight groups, hurrying without stopping to burn or pillage. They avoided using torches to mark their escape route. Their 'trek' took on the speed of a forced march. Two days earlier, at Poix, Airaines and Oisemont, they had stopped after about four leagues. The day before that at Airaines and Oisemont they had covered about five leagues.

That early morning, before daybreak, they had already covered eight leagues, probably passing Saint-Maxent, Tours-en-Vimeu, Acheux and Quesnoy, a road that Edward found suitable, avoiding wooded vales, marshy and uneven ground and the risk of ambushes.

At the break of day, however, the English realised that their forced march had been to no avail. They had reached the edge of the ford only to discover a high tide and an impassable crossing. It was impossible to go any further. Everybody halted.

The French were, of course, behind them, and also opposite on the other bank of the river, and in the dawn light the English could distinguish many people. The situation in which the army found itself was openly dangerous. The tired and nervous soldiers started to grumble, but what could be done? They had to wait.

Philippe's army, albeit hurriedly raised, was huge compared with the English force. It was almost exclusively feudal, gathered at the summons of the sovereign amongst vassals, who provided horses and footsoldiers, and amongst the freetowns, who provided their militia — the commoners, groups of people armed as best they could: sometimes with improvised weapons, more often with boarspears than halberds, and more often with knives than daggers. Peasants and artisans were taken away from their work, dressed in 'battle' clothes, which were to some extent padded and covered with pieces of boiled leather over which the wearer would sometimes attach metal plates.

It was summer and the commoners marched in wooden clogs, or simply went barefoot. Some wore overshoes, their feet covered in pigskin and bound with pieces of cloth.

These common soldiers — who formed a vast forest of boarspears, amongst which a cavalry charge could be halted — had achieved wonders at Bouvines 130 years earlier. They were of value, however, only because there were so many of them. The men were hardly trained and their military role was minimal; they were not easily manoeuvrable and were often late. It was the sheer force of numbers that made them impressive.

THE BLANQUETAQUE FORD

The place name remains to tell us the precise position of the Blanquetaque ford, but there is no trace of it today other than the access path from the south. We do not know how it was reached from the north. The marshes of the Somme that it crossed have been transformed into lakes and ponds over centuries by gatherers of peat. Roger Agache believed that the ford, which must have consisted of raised bedrock like that of Chaussée-Tirancourt, was probably destroyed by the army during the seventeenth century.

The countryside and the water systems were considerably modified during the nineteenth century when the Somme canal and the Paris–Calais railway were built. Penetration by the tides was gradually stopped by silting and a railway embankment across the Somme downstream has totally upset the ecological balance of the valley. Examining the contour lines and knowing that the ford lay between the five-metre contours, we can only estimate its length underwater at less than 2,400 m. A forest existed to the north of the river until the middle of the nineteenth century, the forest of Cantâtre, together with a few other woods that can be seen on old maps. The forest completely covered the horizon, and it is difficult today to imagine the countryside of the fourteenth century, and to assess the extent of this uncrossable gap that was deeply flooded each day by the sea.

In a letter dated 22 January 1390, noted by Louandre, King Charles VI made an allowance to the people of Abbeville to pay for the damage caused by a violent storm during the night of Christmas 1389; the low-lying fields were all flooded and the moat in front of the ramparts of Abbeville was filled with sand. Yet Abbeville today is 25 km from the sea.

33

Moreover, it was August and harvest-time. As Favier rightly remarked, those who were sent to join the army were rarely the most skilful or the strongest; and the knights showed an open disdain for these footsoldiers, who were used as labourers and navvies during the sieges.

In spite of their goodwill and courage, the commoners would never share in the military glory. These footsoldiers were considered to be worth even less than their appearance suggested.

French strength lay in a cavalry equipped with swords, the armoured French nobility. Favier emphasises that the fighting knight of 1346 still had the general appearance of a crusader in Palestine or a warrior at Bouvines, with casque, a shield on his left, a three-metre-long spear under his arm and a large sword within arm's reach. By this date only the helmet had disappeared. The casque was lighter, with a movable visor that could be raised when not in battle. The shield was no longer used to stop blows but rather as a means of parrying them.

The armour was expensive but it was invaluable to the person wearing it. Comprised of iron plate, horn or boiled leather, it was either articulated or sewn depending on the inspiration of the craftsman or armourer. Favier points out that the armour did not protect against a spear blow but from being killed by a horse's hoof or from breaking a limb after being struck by a hoe.

With feet secured in the stirrups during the charge, the knight in a very short gallop threw all his weight and force on the tip of his spear which had an enormous impact (of over a ton). ★

The force of the blow either pierced the target or threw the knight in the air, depending on the skill with which the blow was meted out or received. Combat required great strength, and the immediate proximity of the enemy. It was impossible to hit anything further away than a few steps because the spear was used only once at the point of contact; the sword, a mace or sometimes an axe was then seized.

The help of many squires, and, it would appear, a pulley block, was required to hoist a fully-armoured horseman onto his mount, as was pointed out with much mirth by the English.

The cavalry was thus a shock weapon. What would happen, though, if the attack was scattered, the impulsion lost and the knight thrown to the ground? He could hardly get up. If no one came to his aid and replaced his horse, he would be stranded , a lobster on the sand: a helpless prey to the English pikeman.

The knight, however, was *not* alone. His retainers

★ 'Around 800 kilos of horse, 70 kilos of rider, 40 to 50 kilos of armour and weapons, 50 kilos of saddlery and accoutrements, without forgetting the horse's protective cladding of iron or boiled leather.' M. Guillotel.

bustled around him. A knight's retainer maintained the warrior's weapons and armour, and dressed, prepared and refreshed him. Grooms busied themselves with the great war-horses. Considered large for the period, these horses would, on the contrary, seem small today, standing only 14.2 hands high. They were solid and 'square', weighed around 800 kilos and were of mixed blood. When harnessed and armoured, the horse, although hardly able to gallop, was impressive, and a dense charge of war-horses appeared overwhelming.

When not engaged in battle, the knight used a palfrey, which was a lighter horse of better appearance. Below this came the servants' cobs and the working horses, the invaluable pack-horses or carthorses.

All of these soldiers, knights and retainers made up the large force known as *la lance garnie* ('the garnished spear'). It would have been dangerous to have launched an attack with any one of the separate elements, but together in battle they all fought as one warrior, and

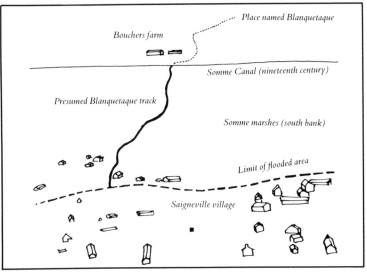

THE VILLAGE OF SAIGNEVILLE

The road to the ford. This was the starting point of the track which led from the south bank to the old ford of Blanquetaque, and which has now disappeared. Roger Agache has discovered medieval fortifications there, as at Boismont. The track today ends at the Somme canal and does not extend on the other side.

35

At the place named le donjon *near to Boismont, on the south bank of the Somme, Roger Agache has identified one of the medieval fortifications of the old Blanquetaque ford. This was probably a tower, perhaps built of wood, surrounding a circular moat that can still be seen from the air and on which trees are now growing. The position was in the old marsh at the limit of firm ground. Roger Agache has also located another defensive fortification near to the village of Saigneville, in the place named* la bastille.

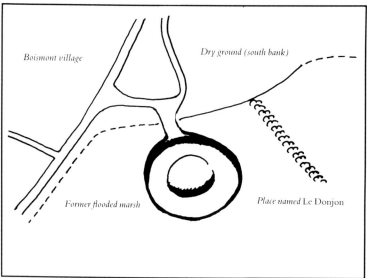

thus created large gaps in the calculations of feudal armies.

The method of fighting used by Philippe's knights was as follows. The knight was a Christian who was not seeking to kill, as were the 'peasants who are afraid'. As far as the knight was concerned, he preferred to capture the enemy and then hold him for ransom. The knight respected his prisoner, his catch. For him it was a question of winning fame for his family by conquering an enemy in the service of his king. He fought from pride at the head of his fief's men, from duty since it was his profession, and from pleasure. What mattered was being where honour could be gained.

On the whole, a knight was a very brave combatant and an ardent warrior but a mediocre soldier, virtually incapable of carrying out a plan that he could not grasp or a manoeuvre different from one which involved accosting the enemy from the front and throwing himself recklessly as soon as possible into the most intense mêlée.

Commoners and knights formed the bulk and backbone of Philippe's army, but he had other divisions which were perhaps more dangerous: these included troops and bands of soldiers, volunteers from all walks of life — penniless nobles, illegitimate sons without a family, landless peasants and exiles without a country — who formed groups and hired themselves out.

Finally there were the mercenaries, German and Genoese pikemen: a minority of professionals. These footsoldiers, who were there to kill and earn their living, did not have a good reputation. Pikemen slaughtered more than they fought and the crossbow was regarded as the weapon of 'cowards'. According to Louandre, the French protested that with this 'treacherous' weapon a 'poltroon' could kill the 'bravest man' — and it was true. The crossbow's short arrows (really bolts, which had small shafts with metallic fletchings) could pierce a suit of armour at a hundred metres. The weapon was so formidable that a synod had previously condemned it. It was not a 'Christian' weapon, and moreover neither training nor physical strength was required to use it. Anybody could do so.

Dangerous as it was, still the crossbow possessed serious faults. It was heavy (about 10 kilos), it clearly did not shoot as far as the longbow, and the shooting speed was five or six times less — two or three shots a minute as opposed to twelve or fourteen. To reload the crossbow, it was necessary to withdraw, put a foot in the stirrup, bend down, use the pulleys and cranks, wind it up, insert the bolt, remove the cocking equipment, stand up again and aim — all without having been able to observe the enemy. It was for this reason that crossbowmen armed themselves for battles on the plain with a type of thick wooden shield behind which they could shelter while reloading. As both hands were full, the shield was kept vertical by a stave. It was complicated, heavy and cumbersome, but it formed part of the carriage and this equipment followed with the supplies.

In sieges, of course, these accessories were not used, as there were parapets. Also at the naval battle of Sluys, only six years earlier, the Genoese crossbowmen (who were then already in the service of France) had at their disposal the ships' decks, the wooden castles and the masts for shelter. Then they had served the king well.

**'If you are engaged on the battlefield endeavour to be with those of the vanguard
You can gain your honour there more than elsewhere.'**
Cent Ballades (fifteenth century).

Below: the priory seen from the north. We can see the buildings where Philippe VI spent the days of 24 to 26 August and where he held his 'great parliament' in the evening of the 25th. To the right is the little church named 'St Nicolas' but which was really St Etienne where the king of France went to mass on the morning of the battle. On the right is the hôtel de ville which still exists, although without a roof. We can recognise the church of St Sepulchre, to the left, although today it has no bell tower. These documents were kindly supplied by Madame Agache, Curator of the Abbeville museum.

As soon as Philippe VI had heard of the English landing, he requested the service of the Genoese again under the orders of the same captains, Carlo Grimaldi and Otto Doria. This division consisted of about 6,000 exiled Castilian or Genoese adventurers, and according to Louandre it had the reputation of combining 'at the same time the most skilful archers and the best sailors in Europe'.

These were the only paid professional soldiers in the mass of men leaving Amiens on 22nd August 1346.

Louandre estimated, in 1844, that in total 'the French army amounted to 100,000 men'. He comments, 'According to Froissart [*Manuscript d'Amiens*] it consisted of 20,000 mounted armoured men and more than 100,000 footsoldiers.'

This was not the opinion of Ferdinand Lot, who wrote, 100 years later, 'The largest contingent at Philippe's disposal was at Aiguillon.★ He was not able to oppose Edward other than with an improvised gathering. The slowness with which the feudal contingents were mobilised was such...that it was impossible for Philippe to have assembled serious forces between 12 July and 26 August... All this points to the French army being smaller in number than the English army.'

The most conservative estimate, he continued, was that of the victor himself, Edward III. In a letter to Thomas Lucy, written at Calais on 3 September (within a week of the Battle of Crécy), Edward says that his adversary had 'more than 12,000 armed men of which 8,000 were gentlemen, knights and squires'. Nobody could have counted them better than the warlord who, during that day, observed them himself precisely to measure their strength. His clerk, Richard Winkley, who was also at Crécy, wrote that there were at least 12,000 knights and 60,000 footsoldiers.

Be that as it may, the French king felt powerful. His army was enthusiastic and each man impatient to fight. An impressive mounted crowd surrounded the king. There were several thousand horsemen, important and not-so-important lords, his own brother Charles, Count of Alençon, the Counts of Blois, Sancerre and Auxerre, Pierre de Bourbon, Jean de Croï, Jean de Conflans, Jean de Vienne, (the archbishop of Reims), followed by his archiepiscopal troops, and Hugues, abbot of Corbie at the head of 500 men, Raoul de Lorraine, the Duke of Bar, and the Duke of Savoie (recently arrived with 1,000 horses). There were knights gathered from everywhere: the army being in Guienne. There were also foreign kings and allies of all countries, many princes of the empire, the Count of Luxembourg, the blind king of Bohemia whose

★ 60,000 men, according to Froissart, a figure that Lot contests.

38

The track which led from the ford of Blanquetaque to Noyelles along the old shore was still called the chemin de Valois *at the start of the nineteenth century and was the track that the French king followed during the morning of 26 August 1346, charging headlong after the English enemy. The English army itself had marched along this track on the previous day. It most certainly has changed but this picture of a rural lane gives an approximate idea of what the roads must have been like in the fourteenth century; none of them were paved except fragments of the old Roman roads. To the right is the first embankment on the north side of the Somme. The marshes lie to the left; they were covered by every tide at the time of the battle of Crécy.*

daughter had married Jean de Normandie, with his son Charles, king elect of the Romans, Jayme the exiled king of Majorca, dethroned by the king of Aragon then taking refuge with Philippe and Louis, Count of Flanders, expelled from his land by his own subjects.

Leaving Amiens very early, Philippe hoped to surprise Edward at Airaines. Alas, forewarned 'by letters from traitors who were in the king's court' the *Goddons* had moved on. On reaching Airaines only the traces of their rushed departure were found, including 'many skewers of meat, bread in the ovens, wine in barrels 'and many tables laid . . .'.

Having passed Airaines, Philippe took up the chase again. The more he advanced the more he could sense the English. He saw the traces of their pillaging everywhere, in animal carcasses and still-smouldering buildings, in the pleas of ruined peasants and in the smoke. Everything indicated the direction the hurried enemy had taken.

On the 24th at 3 am, Philippe reached Oisemont. The English had made tracks only several hours before. They had left with their carts in the direction of Blanquetaque leaving meat and cauldrons still on the campfires.

'Can I cross this ford myself?' Philippe enquired.

'No, my Lord,' replied a knight who was advising the king, 'at this moment the tide is coming in and it will soon be higher than a man.'

The French runners arrived at the Somme just in time to see the last of the English cross. Louandre assures us that the French were only able to reach the rearguard, from which they took baggage and killed a few men.

At the end of this long chase, then, the English had still managed to escape!

Philippe, obviously disappointed and probably at a loss, decided to stop — nothing was urgent any more. Horses were unharnessed and the army set up camp. They took refreshment and 'drank a little'. Philippe himself went to the Knight Templar hostelry where Edward had spent the night. An hour later, when Philippe had reflected on his position and reached his decision, he gave his orders. The army would move off again, footsoldiers behind the horsemen. They took the only path by which it would be possible to continue pursuing the English via Abbeville, which opened its gates to him and where the bridges, 'which were very old and too weak for the carts', were quickly re-inforced.

What had happened? How could the French who held all of the other crossings — Picquigny, Long, Pont-Rémy and Abbeville — have left one crossing unguarded? Even if he knew it was there, Edward should never have been able to cross the ford.

On the previous day, 23rd August, Godemars du Fay, Bailiff of Vermandois, who had been warned about the English manoeuvres, had come to hold the northern exit of the ford. With him were Jean de Picquigny, the Sire of Caumont, Jean de Cange and, as well as mounted soldiers, units from many neighbouring towns (Abbeville, Montreuil, Saint-Riquier, le Crotoy) comprising thousands of armed footsoldiers. There was even a band of militia from Arras and people from Tournai. Froissart, who no doubt exaggerates, records a total of 12,000.

If a letter from an English witness, Michael of Northburg, which was written from Calais within ten days (on 4th September) is to be believed, the crossing was defended by only 500 armed men and 3,000 commoners.

Edward arrived at the southern entrance of the ford at 5 am, before sunrise, at the village of Saigneville. He had to wait three hours for low tide in the midst of what we know to have been a nervous army. At 8 am the water had almost receded and the ford was about to become passable. The impatient Edward gave an order to his marshals, Hugues Spencer, Cobham and the Earl of Northampton, to forge across the river with soldiers and with the best horsemen. The water was still high.

From the northern bank the mounted French knights, on seeing the English approach, decided to throw themselves into the water to fight — under the watchful eye of the footsoldiers — thus losing the

'And there were armed men...with them came the crossbowman of Amiens and Abbeville, of Saint-Riquier and all the crossbowmen from the neighbouring towns. And they were over 12,000.'
Froissart, *CCXVI*.

★ Louandre, whose sources are exclusively French and contrary to Froissart, says that the fight was long. Godemars' troop, driven back on the plain between Noyelles and Port, rallied at Sailly-Bray and fought again. It was perhaps on the ridge of Royon-Soudart, that is 'le rideau du soldat' (the curtain of the soldier), where the French regrouped and, according to Louandre, held out against the attack. In his opinion it was not possible to doubt that many battles took place, because he had verified before 1844 that the name and position of the site and the memories of war had been preserved by tradition.

advantage of their overlooking position. In the receding current, everyone who was fighting was completely soaked and many were drowned. Unseated in the water, a knight in armour disappeared immediately, weighed down by his suit of iron. The English, whose only opportunity this was to break through, managed to advance, crossing the flooded ford and landing on the opposite bank, finally reaching the fields where they positioned themselves for battle. The archers hurried along behind the horsemen. Soon they were ready and they fired.

Froissart explains, 'As soon as the good countrymen that Godemars du Fay had brought with him to assist in guarding and defending the crossing sensed the arrows of these archers and that they would run through them, they all dispersed...turned on their heels and left the gentlemen to fight as best they could.'

Froissart, especially in his first version, clearly supports the English, and gives the impression that the French ran without fighting.

Michael of Northburg quotes 2,000 casualties, and this figure is corroborated by Lavisser elsewhere. 'The English archers fired so strongly and with such unity — it was wonderful.' This means that their volley fire was astonishing in its density and co-ordination.

As at Caen, and no doubt at Poissy, Saint-Just and Oisemont, thousands of soldiers yielded at the first encounter with the new weapon. Neither forewarned nor forearmed to withstand the thick volleys of arrows fired under orders, the soldiers were sitting targets offered up to this fatal hail of thin projectiles.

Under this unremitting shower of arrows, that were watched with such horror by the French, there were above all (as portrayed in contemporary miniatures) a large number of wounded, with pierced shoulders or thighs, who fell in agony. They cried as much from pain as with the terror of suddenly being condemned, prostrate under the deadly hail of arrows, to the mercilessness of the pikemen.

Those who remained standing, even stoical, through the first burst of fire, were staggered by the sight of the rapid losses, of the vast numbers of wounded sustained when the enemy was still so far away. They could see another cloud rising in the distance. The arrows burst into the sky, rose slowly, seemed to hang in the air, and then, in a rush of wind, swooped down in one blow on the waiting soldiers. Each knew he would be transfixed — it seem inevitable. In such a situation, who would choose to stand there and be impaled, with no gain to anyone, when they could run away?

Naturally, they all stampeded away, turning on their tails, and left the gentlemen to fight as best they could. ★

42

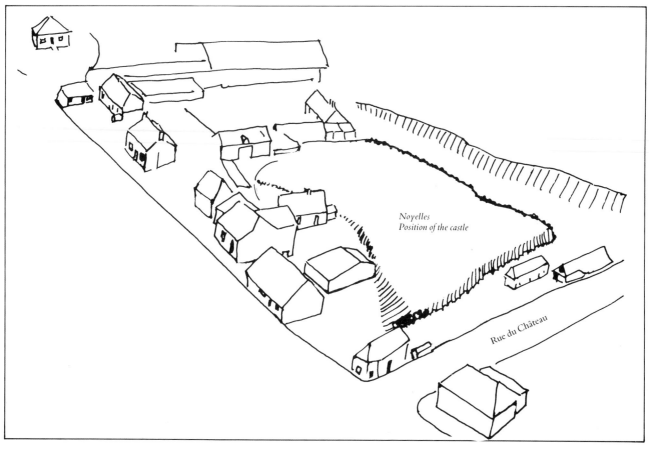

Noyelles
Position of the castle

Rue du Château

Unfortunately, it seemed that the knights were not able to do much to halt the enemy now that, in its turn, the English transport was crossing; besides which, according to Froissart, this crossing of the transport prevented the English from pursuing the defeated enemy. Godemars was seriously wounded and realised that — beaten by the enemy, and without infantry — he could no longer prevent the crossing. He therefore withdrew and left for Saint-Riquier with those crest-fallen knights who survived.[1]

Rothero quotes from the *Meaux Chronicle*, which said that the entire English army 'crossed in an hour'.[2]

Disappointed, Philippe marched towards Abbeville, four leagues from Oisemont. The king mulled over his failure but held Godemars du Fay responsible for not knowing how to hold the river.

In front of Jean de Hainaut, the king affirmed his intention of hanging Godemars. There would be no pardon, no exile, only the noose. Godemars, who heard of this, remained sensibly two leagues away at Saint-Riquier.

Crossing over the bridges and welcomed by its mayor, Colart-le-Ver, Philippe entered Abbeville with the army marching behind him. The crowd of soldiers was so enormous that the town was not large enough, even though it was 'big, sprawling and with adequate lodgings'. Everywhere was occupied by the troops, even the surrounding villages.

The king, for his part, went to stay at the Priory of Saint-Pierre where he spent Friday the 25th, the feast of Saint Louis, the canonised king of France who had died in Tunis 86 years earlier.

New contingents arrived all day long. The army waited particularly for the Count of Savoie and his brother Louis, 'with more than 1,000 lances from Savoie and Geneva'.

Arrangements were made for an early departure the following morning, and no doubt the king indicated the marching orders for the different 'battles', for that evening, after supper, Philippe VI summoned his barons to 'an extensive discussion on weapons'. He addressed them both as their king and as a knight. He quite probably feared the rivalry and dissension between the champions of all these noble families, as they were over-excited at the approach of battle and had come to win glory in their country's service. Philippe begged them all to be 'one to the other friendly, courteous, without envy, hatred or pride'.

Very early the following morning, having attended mass, the French set off again in search of the English.

It was probably about 11 am on 24th August when

1. Froissart notes that he was told that the man who carried Godemars' banner threw it in a bush because it was a hindrance to riding. The English found it there the same day. To lose the banner, especially to the enemy, was, of course, a serious dishonour.
2. If all this is true, Blanquetaque ford was only passable for a short time in the morning on 24 August 1346. Edward III, in fact, began crossing a still-deep river as soon as he could. If we estimate the duration of the fight in the ford to be less than an hour, which is plausible, and if the army crossed it in an hour, it was passable for less than two hours. The French vanguard did, in fact, reach the last of the English but could not give chase, as the water was rising.

Edward III crossed the river. Now he was, he said, back on home ground in Ponthieu, his mother's fief. In one way he was right, even if the English had always had difficulty in extracting obedience from their vassals who waged a permanent silent rebellion. The people of Ponthieu, ruined by England, had done so even more during the previous year; Abbeville and le Crotoy, however, supported by Philippe de Valois, had rejected this burden and chased away the English. In another sense, though, this king who had that day described himself as on 'home ground' was, in fact, on enemy territory. He knew it and he behaved accordingly.

In any event he was free. Philippe had missed the tide, Godemars du Fay had retreated, and the English at last had some breathing space. They took the initiative again. First of all they put themselves in order. They reformed, their banners unfurled, with the vanguard and the marshals leading, the king and his son following, then the rearguard and finally the carts and their guards. Now they were as organised as they had been in Normandy, Vexin and Vimeu.

Froissart relates that with only Canche to pass near Montreuil, ten kilometres from Blanquetaque, they were now heading towards the north, Artois and Flanders.

The English were, however, tired. The troops had been marching since midnight, had already covered

FORTIFICATIONS IN THE PLATON MARSH

At Ponthoile, on the evening of 24 August, the English army had been following an exceptionally long road since midnight — the equivalent of a stage and a half, about 31 km, instead of the 21 to 22 km that it had marched each day during the previous eight days. It had fought at Blanquetaque, burned Noyelles and laid siege to its castle. Froissart tells us that the troops were tired when they set up their bivouacs at 'Labroye', that is, in a fortified place that was necessarily very near to Noyelles where Edward expected to stop. We know that a fortification in earth existed in the marsh at 1,800 m to the north of Noyelles and which Roger Agache, in his Atlas d'archéologie aérienne de Picardie *does not note as dating from antiquity.*

An old map shows an ancienne tour de Pont Dien *of which we know nothing. Perhaps this was the remarkable round structure that Roger Agache discovered when flying over it on a snowy day. This fortification, which perhaps was still used defensively in 1346, is located on the boundary of the dry land to the south of Ponthoile. (Detection aérienne, by Roger Agache, plate 195, fig. 624). Roger Agache says that 'the English archaeologists tend to say that these ringworks are of Norman origin; they are very thick in comparison to the area that they enclose.'*

45

more than an average day's march of over eight leagues and had fought a skirmish. They needed to stop. Edward decided to go as far as Noyelles, which was only half a league away, and his troops would be able to rest in the castle and town.

Edward sent reconnaissance parties ahead to scout, while he marched with the army. Louandre writes that the English were visible from the gates of Abbeville and Saint-Riquier.[1]

Edward arrived at Noyelles in Ponthieu, which resisted. The French fought with courage, say the chronicles, but they succumbed: the town was burnt and the castle besieged. It was not known, of course, that of choice Edward never conducted sieges and avoided castles that held out, only entering by surprise (Caen), by intimidation (Carantan) or if abandoned (Airaines or Poix). What was the surrounded Noyelles going to do?

Catherine d'Artois lived in this castle. She was the daughter of Robert d'Artois, a one-time faithful companion of Edward III. Robert d'Artois was a banished French knight (as was Geoffroy d'Harcourt) who had died in Brittany in Edward's service three years earlier. Like a large part of the French nobility, Catherine d'Artois did not like the Valois king of France but could not forbid the French entry to her fortress. Now she was isolated, and threatened with imminent ruin because of a cause to which she had little allegiance. Catherine had the drawbridge lowered, came out herself, and asked to meet with Edward whom her father had served for so long. She begged him to spare her castle, her people and goods. Then she saw Geoffroy d'Harcourt. Catherine's daughter, Blanche, had married one of Geoffroy's nephews, Jean d'Harcourt; they were therefore related by marriage. She pleaded with him. Edward gave way and the castle was spared.[2]

It was, it seems, a time for generosity. Louandre tells us that it was at Noyelles that Edward paid his debt and, as agreed, gave a hundred gold nobles and a horse to Gobin Agache, who disappeared and was never heard of again.

According to Froissart, the English went on their way without touching either the town or the castle and camped at a site called 'Labroye' that has not yet been identified. The marshals began their raids again. Hugues Spencer took le Crotoy with a unit of cavalry. He entered the town, burnt it, surrounded the castle (which had resisted) and killed 400 French, reached the port and seized the anchored ships. These were the ships from Saintonge and La Rochelle loaded with wine from Poitou and Gascony: a godsend for an

1. Certain English divisions had, therefore, covered about 70 kilometres during the day of 24 August. Of necessity lightly armed, they probably changed horses after crossing Blanquetaque.

2. Louandre notes, in 1844, that only a vast ruined buttress surrounded by several crumbling walls and deep moats remained of the castle. Today the buttress is surrounded by houses and the ruined walls have disappeared (see illustration on p. 43).

Location of the Château du Crotoy, that the troops of Edward III surrounded, but did not take, on 24 August 1346. The castle is an island at high tide. The town around it was at the time a busy port, trading with La Rochelle and Flanders. The castle frequently changed hands and was used as a prison for Joan of Arc in 1430.

All the low-lying land was flooded at high tide during the fourteenth century, excepting Noyelles, Rue and le Crotoy. It was not possible to deploy an army there.

exhausted army. Following his raid, Spencer set off towards the north, taking muddy tracks that were often flooded by the sea, and from which he could not stray for fear of being bogged down in the marshes.

He arrived at Rue, which he burnt, having first taken provisions, since the English army was hungry. 'Their supplies were virtually exhausted,' wrote Michael of Northburg. That evening at Labroye, the exhausted *Goddons* at last rested, ate and drank well.

On the 25th, Edward seems to have taken the wrong route. Was this due to lack of guidance or to new information brought back by the reconnaissance parties and the previous day's raids? Whatever the reason, the king changed his itinerary. Whereas he had been travelling towards Montreuil in the north, that morning he set off towards the east.

Froissart does not explain why, but the reason seems obvious. In the fourteenth century, this shore of the Channel was still very marshy. Some of the high tides flooded the fields, and at high tide the castle of le Crotoy was an island. The estuaries of the Somme, Maye and Authie were lost within enormous un-drained, boggy stretches. Paths (as opposed to actual tracks) criss-crossed the area, and these paths probably changed from year to year. Farms were built from wood, mud and reeds; they were isolated on the occasional hillock, and did not constitute villages.

Waterlogged plains, inhabited by seabirds, stretched as far as the eye could see. Nothing stood out on the bare horizon. To the left was the sea. Ahead to the north it would be foolhardy to use carts or even to deploy troops. Edward, therefore, decided to set off again to the east, to reach firm ground where he could eventually reform his forces for battle: his army was worthless unless it was orderly.

The forest of Crécy, whose boundaries then seemed hardly to have changed since the medieval clearing of land had finished more than a century earlier, stretched to the east. Would Edward fight here? Such a possibility is not mentioned by any of the chronicles,

Crossbow arrows

These sharp points formed the tips of the short crossbow arrows and constituted such dangerous missiles that the church requested their abolition, but to no avail. Such a bolt could pierce any coat of mail, but the missile could only be fired at long intervals: three or four times a minute as opposed to twelve or fifteen for the conventional bow. Moreover, the crossbowman had to shelter behind a heavy shield whilst reloading his weapon. At Crécy he was unable to do so due to the speed of the attack. The English longbow shot further, at a speed four times faster, a lighter arrow that was in theory less lethal but which proved capable of stopping all of the charges of the armed knights. At Crécy, the French had approximately 6,000 crossbows and the English around 5,000 longbows — fairly equal figures. The longbow scattered the crossbowmen with the first exchange and this immediate success decided, to everyone's surprise, the outcome of the battle. The moral effect of the French defeat was so shattering that it overshadowed the technical aspect, which they did not take into account for eighty years.

but it was hardly likely. It was obvious from his advance in Vimeu that Edward wanted to remain on solid ground, avoid covered paths and keep as open a sky above him as he could. The sky was the support of his power: no sky, no archers; no archers, no more English.

Edward probably skirted the forest to the south, since the northern edge was a marsh. The most probable hypothesis is that his route took the wide cultivated corridor that separated the forest of Crécy from other wooded massifs, one being the forest of Cantâtre which still existed in the eighteenth century, when the map was drawn by Cassini.

In this hypothesis, the route would have taken Edward through Sailly-Bray, Nouvion, Forest-l'Abbaye, the sout-east border of the forest of Crécy, and Marcheville, keeping as far away as possible from Abbeville, since it was there that Philippe's army was to be found.

This Edward knew from reconnaissance of the day before. His new itinerary forced him to approach nearer to it before leaving towards the north.

At the end of roughly 21 kilometres, Edward stopped. It was the average duration of a march, but this was probably not the only reason. His men were now exhausted. They had marched without a rest since Poissy. It is estimated that they covered about 230 kilometres in nine days. Their march had become more and more hurried, in a country which was more and more hostile and menacing, in the middle of more and more frequent skirmishes, on land that was less and less predictable. The previous day his troops had been grumbling.

Edward knew the French to be powerful, and nearby. If by a matter of luck, the French stopped that day, allowing Edward to escape the trap of the lowlands, their pursuit could be taken up again the following day. No doubt Edward reckoned that his army could not maintain the pace for much longer. The Flemish allies were still far away, no aid had been foreseen, and no re-inforcements were expected. If the chase lasted much longer, their pursuers would take on the speed of hunters prior to the kill, and they would meet the fate of the quarry. If disunited, the *Goddons* would quickly become a prey for the ruined peasants to finish off.

It is certain that by Friday evening Edward adjudged the risk of fleeing to be greater than the risk of fighting a battle. He stopped and 'explained', but his words were a pretext:

'I will go no further without having seen our enemies,' he said. 'I will wait for them here, for I am in this place by right, inherited from my mother, and I wish to defend it.'

There remained only the choice of site for the now-inevitable confrontation. Edward's last advantage was to be able to decide the time and place. While his army settled down for a rest, Edward sent his best marshals, the most experienced, Warwick, Renauld of Cobham, the Earl of Suffolk and Geoffroy d'Harcourt to choose the site of battle. On the morning of Saturday, 26 August, having explored the district, the nobles were in agreement.

'Sire', they announced, 'this is where we will wait for the enemy, to our advantage.'

'They marched resplendently and in good order with their carts and rode with their banners unfurled, firstly the marshal's vanguard, then the king and his son the prince and, lastly, the rearguard...they feared nothing because they felt the River Somme behind them.'
Froissart, *CCXIX*.

4 THE BATTLE

During the evening of the 25th the news of battle spread through the English ranks: they would fight on the following day. That evening, however, they would celebrate; such was the custom. There were provisions, wine and meat.

Edward invited his barons and all the captains to dine. They enjoyed themselves inside the tents, as did the men outside round their campfires. They sang and guzzled, and then it was over. The officers invited to dine by the king turned in, Edward having advised them to rest well. As for Edward, he went to the private chapel that his chamberlains had erected as usual, and knelt. The night before this decisive battle, Edward commended his actions to God, since he felt he was within his rights, and asked Him 'with affection' to be able to return to England afterwards. Finally Edward went to bed.

The site had been chosen, and on rising each prepared himself for battle. Mass was said before the bulk of the army, and everyone collected their thoughts, for many would not see the end of the day. After mass had been said, it was 'time for eating and drinking'. Finally, the soldiers took up their battle positions; each knew his place and joined it.

The troops, who were now rested, fed, mentally prepared and carefully equipped, settled down calmly, and in a disciplined manner, as they had not had to make an initial march.

How many troops were there? Ferdinand Lot has studied thoroughly the figures of the forces, analysing the *writs* (Edward III's written orders issued when preparing for the Guienne expedition, and preserved in London). He sides with Sir James Ramsey's conclusions.[*] On departure the English had 2,884 horsemen and 7,080 footsoldiers (comprising say 3,580 archers and 3,500 Welshmen). This totalled 9,964 (roughly 10,000).

Edward lost 500 men at Caen, others at Poissy, Saint-Just, Poix and Oisemont, more than 500 at Abbeville, and more at Blanquetaque, Noyelles and le Crotoy; in fact he had lost men at all the sites at which the French, however briefly, had fought them. More must have fallen along the way, exhausted, wounded, or killed in the villages they burnt.

How many able-bodied soldiers remained that morning amongst the English lines? By adding up the divisions — not all of which are known — Sir James

[*] Sir James Ramsey, 'The Strength of English Armies in the Middle Ages', *English Historical Review*, Vol. XXIX 1914, p. 221–227.

Ramsey estimates there were at least 8,200 men.

The supply carts were set out in a closed circle, with only one entrance 'near a neighbouring wood'. This was necessary as the weapon-bearers who supplied the archers with arrows did not have to go too far to collect them. The horses were tethered within this enclosure made from wagons: the English would all fight on foot.

Edward III chose his position at the top of a windmill (no doubt of a height of 8–10 metres, as were all Picardy windmills). From this vantage point he surveyed the whole countryside. His view focused in particular on the Vallée-des-Clercs, and beyond that Fontaine-sur-Maye, the only possible route of the French arriving from Abbeville.

Edward saw to his right the group of 3,800 men under the command of his 15-year-old son, assisted by Geoffroy d'Harcourt, and further to the left the 'battalions' of the Earls of Arundel and Northampton — about 3,000 men. Archers formed the front line, probably interspersed with kneeling pikemen, Welsh lancers and men-at-arms behind. At his feet were the reserves: about 700 men-at-arms and 2,000 archers, with their backs against such an enormous hedge 'that you could not accost them but from the front,' as Froissart said. Each unit was placed in such a way that it could support the other if need be, that is cover it with its fire.

Rothero emphasises that the deployment of the archers is still a subject for discussion. However, we know with certainty[*] that a great number of holes, measuring about 30 cm (1 ft) deep, and the same across, were dug in front of the line. This was a trick learnt from the Scots. These 'fields of holes' broke up the impetus of a charge, the horsemen being obliged to advance cautiously so as not to risk breaking the horses' legs.

The English positions were thus fixed. Edward had no intention of manoeuvring and everything rested on the halting power of the archers. 'The tactic,' Rothero emphasises again, 'was to shake and, if possible, break the French columns before they made contact.' It was hoped that the French would be so severely hammered by the archers that they could easily be pushed back by a relatively reduced division of men-at-arms.

Edward now had his troops deployed but not one Frenchman was on the horizon. The sun was high and we can estimate the time to be about 10 am. What could be done to occupy and maintain the morale of the deployed and motionless troops?

Edward called for a small white palfrey which was elegant, light and sprightly, and he then visited each

[*] 'We do know,' he writes. Lavisse mentioned *trenches*, Lot *abattis*. Froissart, in his first version, says nothing on the subject. Roger Agache's aerial reconnaissance does not reveal old earthworks at this site.

About 600 m behind this tree was the place called Marché-à-Carognes

The road along which the King of France, Philippe VI de Valois, left Crécy for Labroye at a distance of 6 km when night fell on 26 August

The Chaussée Brunehaut can be seen on the horizon; this was the old Roman road leading to Amiens (on the right)

Running from left to right is the Vallée-des-Clercs

The battalion of Northampton and Arundel (at about 200 m)

Edward III's English battalion was held in reserve at this point in front of a thick hedge. The king watched the battle from the top of a mill about 8–10 m high

The supply carts were placed at the rear, in front of a wood, forming an enclosure in which the horses were kept. The varlets carried arrows from this point to supply the archers

THE CRÉCY FIELD OF BATTLE.
Seen from the position of the observation point of Edward III, King of England.

unit. Despite 'his troubled soul', says Louandre, 'Edward III put forward a cheerful face that reassured the most timid'.

The king wore neither armour nor helmet. He was wearing, Louandre informs us, a green velvet doublet intertwined with gold, and he held a white stave in his hand. Intentionally, he stood out amongst the weapons and leather.

Here and there the king stopped to address his men. He preached calmness and silence. He forbade his soldiers to leave the lines during battle to plunder corpses and strip the dead because, as he clearly indicated, if fortune turned against them, all booty would

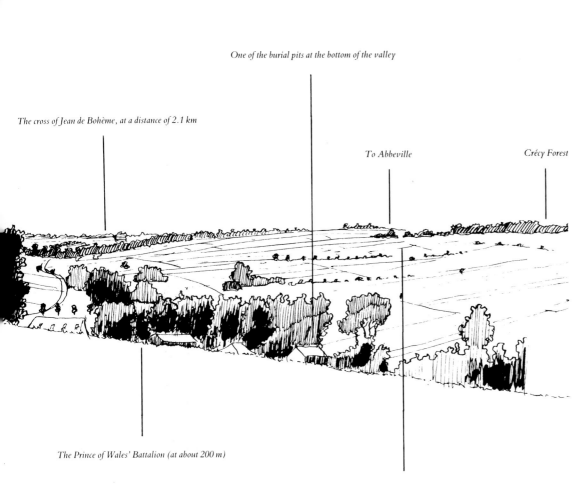

One of the burial pits at the bottom of the valley

The cross of Jean de Bohème, at a distance of 2.1 km

To Abbeville

Crécy Forest

The Prince of Wales' Battalion (at about 200 m)

Point of arrival of the English army on the evening of 25 August,
and of the French army at about 4 pm on the 26th

be useless. Everyone present should do their duty as they were bound. Edward reiterated that he was within his rights against Philippe's claims, and insisted that he would be answerable on his soul. Everybody cheered.

The scene was repeated many times. All eyes followed their king on his white horse, passing through the lines of men on foot. Finally he went back up the hill, towards the windmill. He dismounted and called for his son. The Prince of Wales arrived on foot, accompanied by four knights, John Chandos, Bietremieus de Bruhes, James of Andelée, William Peniels. There, in front of the entire army, the Prince of Wales knelt before his father. The king took his hand, raised him up, embraced him and knighted him.

No one has adequately described the ovation this evoked, which must have been formidable. Froissart, taking up his narrative, only says, 'when the battalions were completely calm', which gives an idea of the enthusiasm shown for the prince.

Edward, who could do nothing but wait, had only one main worry — the need to maintain the morale of his troops. 'The sun was now high; there was no sign of the French; Edward watched out for signs of nervousness', says Favier. 'He disbanded the lines and announced an hour of rest.'

Edward retired to his battalion and ordered that all these people eat at their leisure and drink a while. The men did as they were ordered. They ate and drank at their leisure, then replaced the pots, barrels and provisions on their carts and returned to their positions as ordered by the marshals. Then they all sat on the ground, helmets and bows in front of them, 'resting in order to be fresher and more alert when their enemy came'.

Midday approached as the seated English army waited.

Abbeville, Saturday 26 August. The day had not yet begun, but within the town everyone was up. King Philippe had already heard mass at Saint-Etienne, and the trumpets had been sounded in the streets. Already equipped, both nobles and footmen left immediately, 'without orders, not waiting for each other'. The king was in a greater hurry than anyone else. 'Never had one seen a man leave so early for battle!' Dom Grenier even says that Philippe departed from Abbeville in such a hurry that he left several pieces of artillery behind because he feared being held back during the march!

Where were the English?

It seems that no one in the French army really knew but, in any event, the French were chasing them — and they took the wrong route.

Ferdinand Lot says that Philippe took a route 'that passed to the west of the forest of Crécy'. Arriving at Braye (Sailly-Bray?), Philippe learnt that the enemy had passed the forest, so 'he took the Roman way'. Lot, no doubt, is mistaken, but he is certain that Philippe was floundering. Louandre found out why: when they were in Abbeville, the day before, they had seen smoke coming from Noyelles, le Crotoy and probably also Rue. That morning Philippe therefore hurried towards Noyelles. If he could drive the *Goddons* against the sea and the marshes he would

'Philippe's army was divided into four sections, the first under the orders of the grand master of the crossbowmen, the second under those of the Count of Alençon, the third under those of the king, the fourth under those of Jean de Hainaut.'
Chronique de Flandres.

succeed in completing a manoeuvre that had failed at Vimeu.

Louandre believes that Philippe followed the sandy path that Edward had taken two days earlier. At the beginning of the nineteenth century, the people of Noyelles still called this road 'the Valois path'.

'Why?' asked Louandre.

'Because it is the path that Philippe de Valois took,' he was immediately told.

L'Histoire des Mayeurs d'Abbeville recounts that Philippe's army made its final arrangements in the plains of Titre, plains that it would in fact have had to cross when coming from Noyelles or Sailly, setting out on the tracks of the English, which led to Crécy. This itinerary, therefore, seems to tally with that suggested by other authors.

But where were the English?

After a 'long moment', as they were already far from

Plan of Battle
Composition and Distribution

	The Black Prince	Edward III	Earls of Arundel and Northampton
According to Froissart (14th C) 15,000 men approx.	1,200 men-at-arms 4,000 archers	1,500–1,600 men-at-arms 4,000 archers	1,200 men-at-arms 3,000 archers
According to J. Ramsey (1914) over 8,200 men	800 men-at-arms 2,000 archers 1,000 Welsh	700 men-at-arms 2,000 archers	500 men-at-arms 1,200 archers + Welsh
According to C. Rothero (1981) over 10,700 men	1,000 men-at-arms 2–3,000 archers 1,000 Welsh	700 men-at-arms 2,000 archers	1,000 men-at-arms 3,000 archers + Welsh
Principal officers	Harcourt Warwick Oxford Thomas Holland Lord Stafford Lord Burghersh John Chandos	The King	Sir Mortimer Miles Stapleton Wilhoughby Bishop of Durham

The English army was divided into three 'battles'. Opinions differ on their numerical importance and their composition. Rather than take sides on this subject, estimates from three historians, Froissart, Ramsey (quoted by F. Lot) and C. H. Rothero have been given (although it is clear that Froissart over-estimates the numbers).

The assumed situation of the French forces at 1900 hours on the 26th of August.

Sunset, about 1900 hours on 26 August (1).

Edward's mill (2).
Thick hedge.

Crécy-granges farm (3)
(at 800 m). English supply carts,
Edward III's tent.
French hospital on August 27.

Forces in reserve (4).
Black Prince.
Northampton.

Area dug with holes in front of the English
line (5).

Range of English arrows (6).

Genoese troops (7).
Philippe VI's army.

Crécy (8).

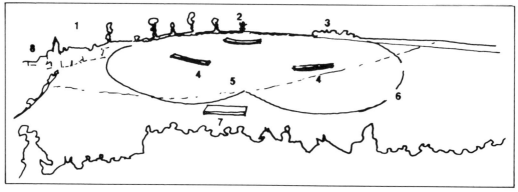

There is no reliable and precise illustration of the English archer in 1346. We nevertheless do possess a fairly large number of miniatures of the fifteenth century which depict them. These miniatures are contemporaneous with the documents that they accompany and are therefore dated about a century after the battle of Crécy. A few of them give an approximate idea of the archer in action and it is felt that it is of interest to include them. The principal difference from the English archer lies in the helmet — the archer of 1346 wore an iron hat and probably no armour.

the town, a counsellor addressed the king, 'Sire, it would be wise if you sent horsemen on in front to acquaint themselves with the enemy's numbers.'

In front of the enormous army ('so numerous that it took over half a day to leave Abbeville', says Froissart), four experienced knights rode away: the Moisne of Basle (le Monne de Basèle in French, the Monk of Bazeilles according to George T. Diller), the lords of Beaujeu and Noyers and Louis of Spain. They pushed ahead at a trot, following the edge of the woods until they discovered the enemy. For better observation, the knights approached to less than an arrow's flight away, but the English, who did not detect them, remained sitting.

Having seen the enemy, the French knights returned. They had noted the order of the English and the disorder of the French. Coming back they met French troops on foot, some with and some without horses, everyone in disarray.

'Why are you marching like that, you madmen, without marshals' banners. You will lose. The enemy is in front of you!'

The troops passed by regardless.

Finally the knights reached the king, who was surrounded by the Counts of Alençon, Flanders and Blois, the Duke of Lorraine, Jean de Hainaut, de Montmorency, and a gathering of lords, who all stopped. The Moisne of Basle submitted his report of three units, in fixed positions, and related the apparent waiting of the English. As he was pressed to speak by the king, Moisne gave the advice to halt and try to instil some sort of order into the army. 'It will be too late to attack by the time the last soldiers have joined the front and the battalions have formed properly. It is already 3 o'clock in the afternoon. After mass tomorrow, with your troops well organised, you can go into battle in a positive manner.'

The king seemed shaken. He consulted his brother and some of his barons, and then agreed. He sent an order to the standard-bearers to halt, via two marshals; one was despatched to the front, the other to the rear. At the front they obeyed.

Behind, in utter confusion, they refused. The troops continued, cheering and announcing that they would go on until they found themselves at the front.

'Stop, standard-bearers. In the name of the king, God and Saint-Denis, halt!' But these orders were to no avail and the troops marched on. Those at the front, on seeing the rearguard arrive, thought the army was continuing and set off again. They also wished to remain at the front. 'I am first and I will remain first,' was the attitude described by Froissart.

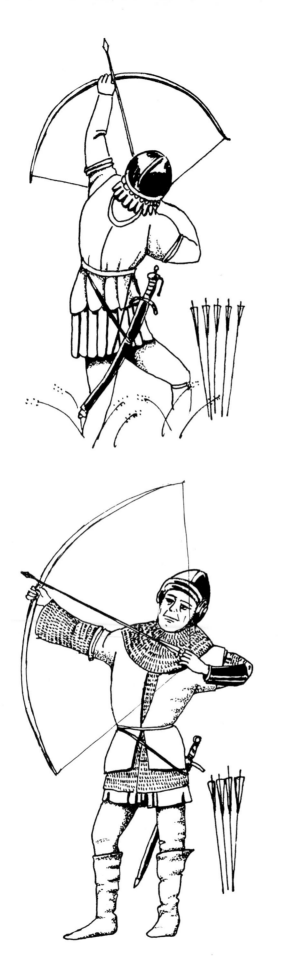

A. *English Chronicles. End of the fifteenth century. This is a right-handed English archer holding his arrow on the left side of the bow. The five arrows placed vertically into the ground near to his hand allow him to fire them more rapidly. He is wearing no armour other than his helmet. He is wearing his sword on his right-hand side which is unusual for a right-handed man and is probably an invention of the painter.*

B. *English Chronicles. End of the fourteenth century. This left-handed archer is holding his arrow on the left-hand side of the bow, which would be impossible in reality. He is wearing his sword on the left, which is also impossible. He is wearing a worn coat of mail which is very realistic with its frayed right sleeve. The left sleeve is missing and has been replaced by a brassard. A second coat of mail is laced to his light helmet, or basinet, on the top of his jerkin. He is wearing a shirt, hose and boots and his arrows are stuck in the ground.*

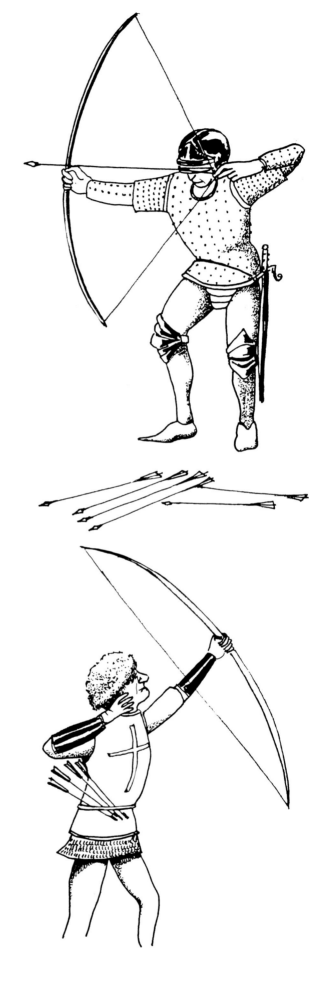

C. Froissart's chronicles. Fifteenth century. Crécy. This English archer is also left-handed and is wearing a helmet, a studded leather shirt, a coat of mail, a studded velvet jacket, and metal knee-pieces which are frequently illustrated in miniatures. These are completed by leather shoes and tight-fitting breeches; his genitals alone appear to be protected by a guard. The arrows with long feathers are simply laid on the ground. The sword is on the left side.

D. Charles II's Prayer Book. Fifteenth century. The bowman in this original illustration seems to be wearing gauntlets. His chapel de fer or iron hat is covered with red cloth. He is wearing the white cross of France stitched to his shirt. This emblem was increasingly used in opposition to the English cross, which was red. The man is carrying four arrows in his belt. He is wearing a coat of mail and metal brassards, but is carrying neither sword nor knife. He is not carrying a quiver, like most of the archers illustrated in miniatures.

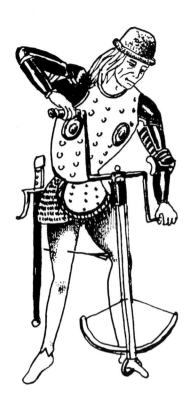

E. Froissart's Chronicles. Fifteenth century. Crécy. This Genoese crossbowman is winding up his weapon without taking the trouble to take shelter. He is wounded, with an arrow through his right thigh. He is wearing armour on his arms and a coat of mail under a studded cloth jacket. His helmet in the form of a chapel de fer *seems to be covered with felt; he is carrying a sword on his right side.*

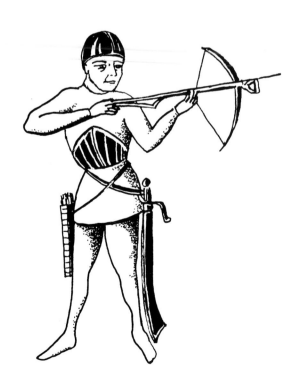

F. Froissart's Chronicles. Fifteenth century. Crécy. This crossbowman is right-handed. He is carrying a quiver on his right side which is well filled with bolts and, on his left side, a long sword for close combat. His only armour is a helmet and a corselet. We can see a long trigger under the weapon with which he fires the bolt. In this case, it is a kind of light arrow.

Philippe's words given the previous evening at Saint-Pierre advising modesty and courtesy had fallen on deaf ears. The advance of the French army was no more than a collective demonstration of armed men. They had no fighting strategy, no discipline, no plan; they just ploughed on, jostling each other. First and foremost they wanted to shine.

The sturdy rustics, clamouring together, were so certain of an easy victory and felt so confident in their numbers, re-inforced by the allied contingents, that they were drunk with bravery. That day at Lamotte-Buleux almost every language could be heard — French, Picard, German, Italian, Czech. But they had no leader and the majority of the troops followed closely on the vanguard. The marshalls gave up, overwhelmed, and, according to Favier, Philippe VI de Valois found himself 'propelled into a battle that he had wanted, whilst the majority of his troops were still spread out along the road'.

Be that as it may, the French advanced along the *Chemin de l'armée* ('the road of the army'), which still retains this name, then suddenly halted. There they were — the English: orderly, silent and motionless.

On seeing this noisy rabble arrive, the *Goddons* simply stood up. They watched the approach of the sprawling crowd.

The first men halted. The French now had to organise themselves, form groups, and get ready. Where were the banners?

The troops were shoving from behind, and a dense crowd gathered. Some wanted to advance but others prevented them. 'Let's stay here,' a few shouted. 'Let's wait for the king and his array! The marshals said so!' But no one was listening. The roads as far back as Abbeville were packed with troops, a vast number of footsoldiers, pikemen, men-at-arms, knights, squires, horses, carts, weapon-bearers and grooms. It was an uncontrollable wave of people who often scarcely understood each other, and whose only laws, apart from the king's service, were the orders of their own lords. They were from Île de France, Rouen, Amiens, Rheims, Vexin and Normandy, each with his own dress, language, weapons and habits. They were all in the same army, but very different from each other.

As soon as the troops arrived in front of Crécy, at the edge of the forest, and saw the well-organised blocks of English, they shouted more or less in unison, 'Death to the English traitors. They will never return to England!'

The French crossed the stream of Maye (which was then probably more marshy than it is today), and many wended their way past the village of Fontaine.

Two views of the same bronze horseman in the Bargello museum in Florence. Although Italy was already in advance of the other countries of Europe in the manufacture of armour, this horseman is a good illustration of what might have been a well-equipped man on horseback at Crécy. We can see an epaulette on his right shoulder which is not part of the armour but probably a heraldic sign, and is perhaps made of leather. The shield, the lance and the sword are restorations of the nineteenth century.

The armour worn by knights during the fourteenth century was undergoing a change. The old crusader's heaume or pot-en-tête was still very widespread. It rested on the shoulders and was worn over a close-fitting steel cap or 'basinet'. The camail, which was lowered when fighting, was still a rare novelty. Over his hauberk (a tunic of ring or chain mail), the knight often wore a cotte de plates (a breast-plate made of metal strips sewn to a leather jacket) or a pièce d'Allemagne, an iron breastplate which was roughly shaped. A tunic covered the whole.

The man may have worn brassards on the forearm, in the form of simple tubes of beaten iron, and small round protective pieces on the knees and elbows.

The most widely worn protection was still only pieces of leather boiled in oil and shaped. The leather may have been reinforced with studs or pieces of horn and was painted. These leather garments were the first line of defence of the body.

Pieces of armour in beaten iron were still rare on the field of battle in Picardy. The garments and armour worn by Ulrich de Werdt, whose recumbent figure is shown above, is a good illustration. This knight died in 1344 and we know that he had his effigy sculpted during his life. His shield used to rest on his basinet but it disappeared in 1792. His head lies on his heaume. The reader is referred to the remarkable study by Charles Buttin on the weapons and armour of knights of the middle of the fourteenth century (Edition Istra, Strasbourg, 1925).

64

They amassed, jostling each other, their backs to Estrées-les-Crécy, facing the dry Vallée-des-Clercs that separated them from the enemy.

The French army marked time. Those in the lead had walked about 30 kilometres. It was mid-afternoon and they were doubtless hungry. The sky clouded over. The French had stopped and lost time. Now they lined up and regrouped, while shouting to each other, each using his own initiative. Finally the French army found themselves in more or less three units. The first consisted of Genoese mercenaries, the second ranked behind the Count of Alençon, the king's brother, and the third gathered behind the king himself, with King Jean de Bohème and the other foreign princes. The Flanders chronicle states that there was a fourth unit led by Jean de Hainaut. There was also the unruly crowd, still advancing, although it was sometimes very far behind.

What must Philippe have thought of this excited rabble who served him yet ignored his orders? The king advanced with his men and then, like them, lost his head upon seeing the enemy. 'As soon as he saw the English,' relates Froissart, 'his blood boiled because he hated them so much!'

Incensed with anger, Philippe lost all resolution and forgot Moisne's advice, and he gave the order to

attack. Moreover, the onslaught was to be headed by the Genoese crossbowmen!

The Genoese, who probably totalled 6,000 men (15,000 according to Froissart), were tired. They had walked all day, each carrying 40 kilos of bows, quivers and bolts. They should have been deployed in an orderly formation under a marshall's orders, and here they were — totally exhausted and without protection — being sent to launch a frontal attack. The big wooden shields that protected them during combat were still on carts far to the rear, as Gilles de Muisit, a contemporary writer, emphasises. The Genoese complained; they wanted to wait. This news reached the Count of Alençon who, in his turn, became angry. He cried, 'You see? Such a bunch of ruffians are hardly worth the bother. They are fit only for the table! Let's kill them all!'

Then large drops of August rain began to fall. The fields and pastures turned into a muddy and slippery surface under the feet and hooves of the trampling army. It was a heavy storm, with thunder, lightning and high wind. In the heavy shower that drowned everything, the countryside was no longer visible. Nothing was distinguishable at 50 metres.

Eventually the rain eased off, and finally stopped. The sun appeared from behind the clouds in the west, above the English. Now that they were in the shadow of the hill, and the French were hindered by the evening sun, the English were hardly visible. The storm passed over.

It is said that a large flock of crows flew between the armies, which some saw as a sinister omen. The Genoese stopped grumbling and prepared themselves. Naturally, they fought in the Genoese manner, and advanced shouting, as ordered, for that was how it was done at home when attacking an enemy. The enemy here, however, could not care less and replied to each clamour, being now within earshot. The Genoese crossbowmen tightened their weapons and fired. Bolts flew and the battle began.

The English archers took a step forward and, under orders, fired in their turn. The volley fire rose, and then hailed down on the Italian mercenaries. Without armour or shield, they had nothing to protect them from the arrows that fell so thick and fast from the sky 'that it seemed like snow'. The Genoese had never before met such organised firing on flat terrain. Froissart emphasises that when they felt these light arrows pierce their arms and chests and wound their faces, arrows which came from even further than they themselves could shoot, out of reach of their own weapons, they began to disperse.

Caen, Blanquetaque, Crécy — it was the same story all over again. Many fell wounded and cried out. Others, already turning their backs, fled as if powerless and ran blindly towards the French lines seeking shelter. However, they found no refuge, as they were surrounded by French men-at-arms.

There was utter scorn for these 'ruffians', these paid footsoldiers, these Italians who uttered such strange cries. Philippe and the Count of Alençon, furious at

The garments can be seen clearly on the man in the illustration below. Over his coat of mail he is wearing a jacket in leather reinforced with strips of iron studs to which his weapons, dagger and sword, are attached by chains that cross through the gussets of a second jacket which is laced on the front and covers the whole. The axe seems to be a restoration made during the nineteenth century. We can see that the man in the illustration on the right is wearing knee pieces and is carrying a heaume held by a chain, and a round shield.

seeing their mercenaries fleeing, issued a ridiculous and monstrous order.

'Kill the footsoldiers! Kill the footsoldiers! They are hindering us and are blocking the way without reason.'

So the French began to kill the Genoese — allies murdering each other. Was it over quickly? — probably not, for the Genoese were excellent troops, known throughout Europe as excellent crossbowmen and sailors,★ and they defended themselves.

During their flight, some threw down their crossbows, but others kept theirs. The Genoese no doubt used these against the French knights. At a short distance a bolt would pierce any armour. Those who no longer had a crossbow still had sword or dagger, and these they used to defend their lives, cutting the horses' hocks and the throats of the fallen men-at-arms.

As many died in this battle as in any other, possibly even more, since the English archers continued to fire on this set-to, and an uninterrupted hail of arrows showered down. 'Not one arrow missed', says Froissart. Many were wounded without knowing from where the blows came.

It was about 7 pm. The Genoese were either dead or had flown. The battle of Crécy had begun.

It was, however, effectively already lost and even in the heat of the battlefield many of the French already suspected this. The English, in particular, thought so as soon as they saw the disordered crowd arrive in front of them. They became sure when they saw Philippe's army start to kill each other.

For the French cavalry, however, their battle had not yet begun. Now it was the turn of the knights, chargers, lances and frontal attacks of the charge and side arms. Now the world would see what a French knight with a name, a weapon and in the presence of a king was made of.

The chargers took up their positions and closed their ranks; visors were lowered, and then lances in their turn were lowered. It was the hour of the nobility, and squires and manservants stayed behind. The armoured mass set off, amidst neighing, at the battle trot. The war-horses never moved very fast.

The knights were now only amongst their own kind. They knew they were being watched and that on their shields the coats of arms would be seen. This long mass of horsemen, this lengthy, bristling line, advanced towards Edward III's army.

It was probably somewhere between 7 and 8 pm when the first French charge slowly surged forward on the still-green pasture, past the Genoese corpses. The

'And so they came, valiant men, for honour and to acquit themselves well, riding forward and not knowing they were going to die.'
Froissart, CCXXV.

★ It is for this reason that the version which claims that the Genoese could not have anticipated that the rain would slacken their crossbow strings seems unlikely; for every sailor knows that water is wet! On the other hand, what they perhaps did not know was that it is difficult to load a crossbow in mud. The mechanism will jam and the exit channel of the bolt lose all firing accuracy if it is not completely smooth. In any event, the Genoese weapon did not shoot as far as the English longbow (150 metres as opposed to 250 metres, as estimated by Viollet-le-Duc).

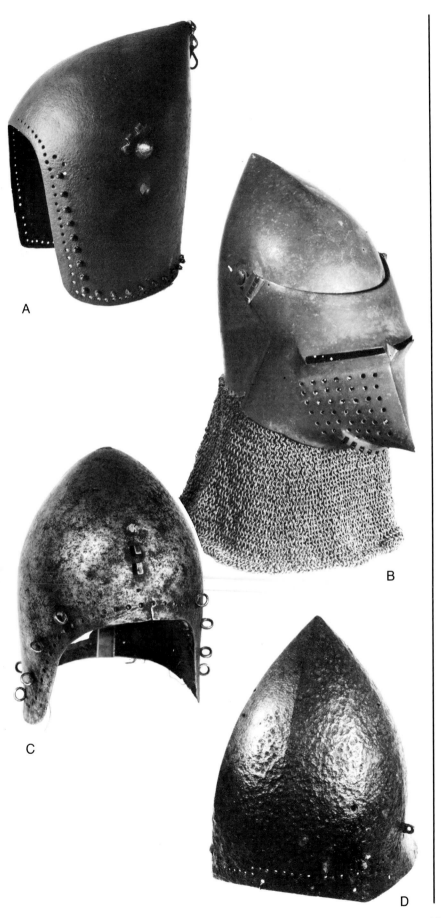

A

B

C

D

A. This basinet with visor of the end of the
sixteenth century comes from a church of
Orléans where it was believed to be a relic of
Joan of Arc. It is at present in the
Metropolitan Museum, New York. Its shape
can be compared with that of older basinets.
B. This remarkable helmet of the sixteenth
century still has its camail or neckguard in ring
mail. It is kept at Chartres and there is no
doubt of its royal origin. The decorations
around the camail have been torn off; perhaps
they were in gold. M. Reverseau, Curator of
the Musée de l'Armée, says that it was
completed by the ribs of a mitre until the
nineteenth century. This helmet, which may
be of Italian style, is probably a gift of King
Charles V.
C. A basinet in forged iron, at the Museum of
Saint Etienne. Note the lacing ring
(vervelles) of the coat of mail which is
exceptionally wide in this case. A device on the
front is designed to hold a piece of armour for
the face.
D. A basinet of conical shape,
contemporaneous with the battle of Crécy, kept
at the Musée de l'Armée in Paris.

THE BLACK PRINCE

According to the English writer, Christopher Rothero, the name 'Black Prince' did not appear before 1569 in Grafton's English Chronicles and there is no previous mention of his name or of the history of the black armour that the prince of England was said to have worn at Crécy.

Froissart gives us full details of the fight in which this sixteen-year-old took part, commanding the troops on the right wing. Jacques d'Estracelles led a charge of French horsemen in the direction of the Prince of Wales by order of the Count of Alençon, brother of Philippe VI, despite his own pessimism about the outcome. Quite unexpectedly, the French penetrated the English defences. The Prince fell from his horse and his banner carrier, Richard de Beaumont, of Norman origin, covered him with his standard and successfully defended him by sword. It is said that Geoffroy d'Harcourt, who had been told to take care of the Prince, then asked the Earl of Arundel to drive off the approaching French.

Louandre tells us that 'all indications show that they were charging up the Vallée-des-Clercs'; Villani says 'the road was covered by the bodies of Genoese troops and dead or wounded horses in great numbers. French troops advancing in disorder increased the confusion and smothered each other. The English on the hillside only had to discharge their arrows randomly to be certain of killing.'

The brave d'Estracelles died with his throat cut. The next day and as a recompense for his courage, the young Prince Edward was awarded by his father the plumes taken from the helmet of Jean de Bohème together with the German motto Ich dien, *which the Princes of Wales still wear today.*

THE SEAL OF JEAN DE LUXEMBOURG, KING OF BOHEMIA

Jean de Luxembourg, King of Bohemia, studied in Paris and his first love was for France. He was elected king of Bohemia in 1310, and remained there. He sent his son Wenceslas to Paris, having him called by the more suitable name of Charles.

The King of Bohemia often came to Paris, either as a pilgrim (Rocamadour), or for tournaments, wasting the riches of Bohemia where it appears that he was little loved. He took part in the crowning of Philippe VI in 1328 and then in an expedition against the Flemish. His daughter married the Duke of Normandy, son of the King of France. After the death of his first wife, he married again in 1334 a daughter of the Duke of Bourbon. He was therefore very close to the French royal family. He visited Prague in 1337, and Montpellier in 1339 for medical attention for his eyes, as he was slowly becoming blind. He fought at Crécy with 500 Bohemian horsemen. It is said that he defended Pont-Rémy on 23 August. His war cry was 'Prague'.

His son, Charles, was also at Crécy, but left the battlefield before the disaster; Favier notes 'one does not risk the crown of the holy Empire on the rough roads of Picardy'.

Charles was elected King of the Romans, Emperor, and King of Bohemia in his turn; he married Blanche, sister of Philippe VI, and leaves the memory of a very good king closely attached to France. He introduced French architecture, arts and customs to Prague. The old kingdom of Bohemia was absorbed during the seventeenth century in Austria, and today belongs to Czechoslovakia. The families of the knights of Bohemia who died in the service of France at Crécy had all disappeared in 1850, except one (L. Léger).

The French did not commemorate the 600th anniversary of the battle in 1946 and no more did the English, for obvious reasons. On the other hand, a number of Czechs came to visit the scene of the death of Jean de Bohème, one-time sovereign of Prague.

To try to give a precise description of a battle waged with cold steel in the open country more than six centuries ago might even be considered reckless. The attempt, however, deserves to be made as an approximation based on existing documents, studies of place names and of the site, tests of arrow flight and observation of aerial photographs.

1. The place named 'Edward's Mill'. There is no mill here now but it is known that the king's observation point stood here. The battlefield was surrounded by a 'thick hedge' on the north-east side which protected the rear of the English forces.

2. A stepped embankment, which still partially exists, served as a position for the English reserve around the king. Froissart says that it covered the other units by firing arrows

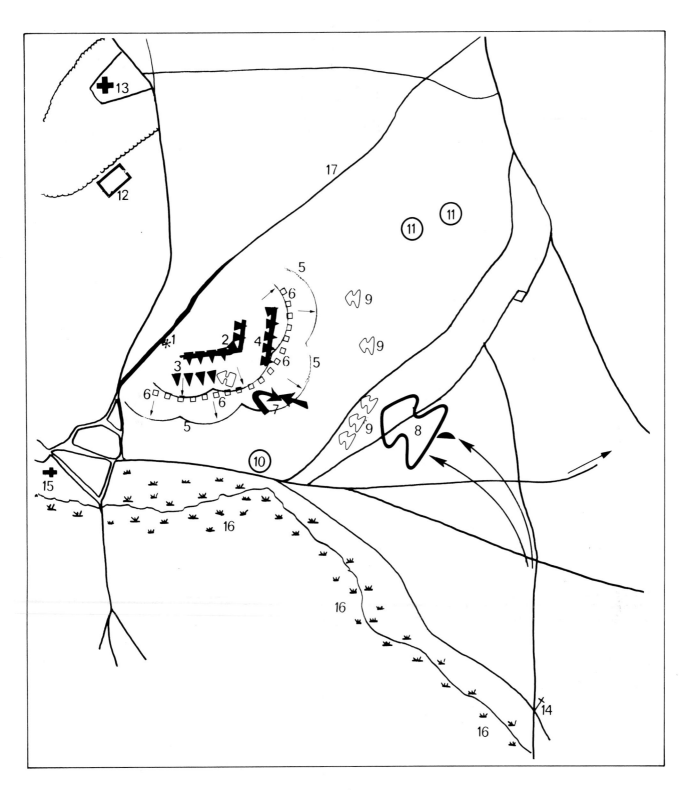

from the English bows that could hit a target at 200 metres. Two battalions were placed in this protected perimeter.

3. The Prince of Wales' Battalion. The gradient of the ground suggests that he may have used an embankment as support point but there is no trace of this at present, even from the oldest air photographs taken before the stadium was built in 1947.

4. The most recent vertical photograph taken by the IGN (French National Geographic Institute) clearly shows traces of a track which has today disappeared, between 10 and 17. This photograph also reveals a deep ridge at 4 (an embankment or sunken track?), the only contour in the defensive area and which is in all probability the position of Northampton's battalion.

5. Approximately the dangerous zone for the enemy where it would have received the concentrated fire of the English arrows.

6. The English built a line of defence within this zone, consisting of square holes of sides about one foot long, intended to break the cavalry charges. There remains no trace of these holes which, according to C. Rothero, was a trick learned in Scotland.

7. A fratricidal combat took place in this dangerous area, under the fire of the English archers, when the Genoese crossbowmen poured back and were massacred by the French troops.

8. The major part of the French troops were facing the west and the setting August sun. Philippe VI would normally have stood at the highest point of the ground to watch the battle.

9. The Vallée des Clercs extends from 10 to 11. The fifteen or sixteen French charges started from this valley, successively but unsuccessfully. The least unfortunate of them reached the Prince of Wales' battalion where it was destroyed (3).

10. The position of a burial pit which was still visible in 1840, according to Louandre. This is probably where the bodies were buried. There is no trace of the great fire made of piled supply carts and in which the English burned the weapons that they did not carry away.

11. The place named Ch'marche a carognes. We can now clearly see traces of at least two pits against the uniform grey of the farming land although they were invisible on the first aerial photographs — the fields were smaller then. It was probably here that the carcasses of the hundreds of dead horses were buried.

12. The English sheltered their horses in an enclosure formed of their supply carts. Records say that the enclosure was protected by a wood, and it must have been near to the battle because the varlets ran to and fro incessantly to supply the archers with arrows. The tents of the king and of his marshals were probably placed in this enclosure or in the immediate vicinity. The position indicated is the most probable but it is totally hypothetical.

13. The farm of Crécy-granges which then depended on the Benedictine abbey of Valloires. The monks set up a temporary hospital there on 27 August and carried to it the wounded survivors of the battle of the previous day. Those who died in the hospital were buried in an enclosure. The memory of this cemetery is maintained by tradition with a corner of hillocky pasture land that has never been ploughed. The surface around this field and within the surrounding wood can be simply scraped to reveal traces of the monks' enclosure consisting of a wall in white stones.

14. The cross of Jean de Bohème. Ballandra doubts, with others, that the cross was built at the time of the battle; it might have only indicated the boundaries of the parish before it was consecrated to the memory of the king. It is located on the edge of the 'army's track' on which Philippe's army arrived.

15. The church of Crécy-en-Ponthieu. A number of great French nobles were buried in this church, but it was destroyed in 1433. There are no traces of the tombs.

16. The marshy zone of the Maye river, which was much wetter then, forms the south boundary of the battlefield.

Side view of the battlefield, as seen from the south.

74

shadows were lengthening. 'When the battle began, it was already very late.'

Night falls at about 10 pm at the end of August. The repeated charges were to last more than two hours. No one knows exactly what took place and Froissart does not mention it: he only relates anecdotes. The next day they would count the dead. There would be no prisoners; this 'battle' was one long massacre.

The 'flower of chivalry', experienced soldiers who were trained in battle, highly motivated, keen, well-equipped, numerous and spirited, fell in their thousands before a handful of English peasants. Who won? — from the evidence, the victor was the new weapon. Courage could change nothing of this brutal fact. Rapid-firing weapons, well supplied, dense and skilfully used, inflicted defeat well before hand-to-hand fighting even commenced.

If the armoured knights were not themselves hit, then the horses were struck by the thin arrows that penetrated their breasts, their quarters and their heads or dangled from their flanks like banderillas in the flanks of fighting bulls. The horses started to neigh, slowed down, panicked and collapsed; they were then jostled by those who followed after, and trampled on, dragging other animals down. The knights fell with their horses. Under this hail of arrows, the squires could not reach the knights to provide a fresh horse, so the knights remained where they had fallen.

Favier says that the English archers fired on sight in the falling darkness as the French knights collapsed along the length of the hedges. This meant farewell to the hope of achievement in battle: the French cavalry had not even reached the enemy.

Nevertheless, the knights advanced resolutely under this hail of iron. Other charges followed the first; new groups of horsemen lunged forward, but against the new weapon the methods of classical battle, those of Hastings, Bouvines or Antioch, were useless. The French soldiers advanced to die in their thousands in front of their lines, simply to prove they were brave. They succeeded: no one has ever doubted their suicidal fearlessness.

Their inability to advance and fight, even on foot, showed that the power of impact of the English arrow was such that it penetrated, however slightly, the French armour. Thoroughly trained to fight on foot and convinced of their indisputable superiority, these passionate fighters would certainly have pursued their advance if they had not been hit before even falling from their horses.

The staves of the Welsh pikemen would have been broken by one blow from the swords of these

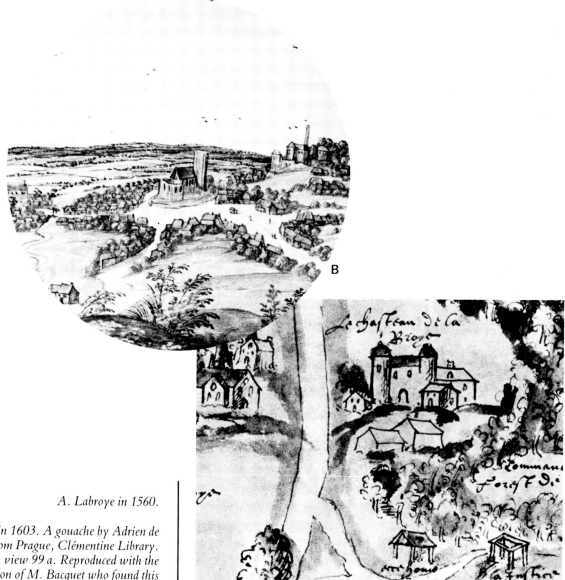

B

A

A. *Labroye in 1560.*

B. *Labroye in 1603. A gouache by Adrien de Montigny, from Prague, Clémentine Library. Vol. 23/A9, view 99 a. Reproduced with the kind permission of M. Bacquet who found this remarkable illustration.*

armoured men, if the latter had not already been neutralised on the spot. Philippe VI's soldiers had to accept one overwhelming fact: in 1346 the English longbow dominated all other weapons, both offensive and defensive.★

For one moment the French thought they were going to be able to jostle the English. A strong party of French horsemen, led by Jacques d'Estracelles, succeeded in reaching the enemy, having survived the murderous arrow fire without collapsing, and having crossed the 'field of holes'. It seemed that side arms would now reclaim their rights. The party marched towards the Prince of Wales, directly threatening him.

The English took fright. Thomas of Norwich ran to the windmill to warn that the young Edward was in a dangerous position, but the king had already seen all and did not consider the situation serious.

'How is he?' The king asked.

★ The author thanks M. Reverseau, curator of the *Musée des Invalides,* for this vital addition to the understanding of the disaster in 1346.

C

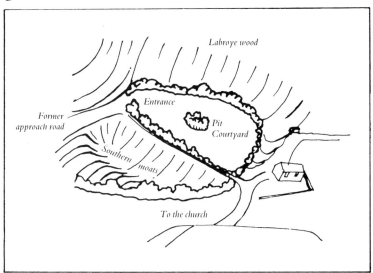

D

C. Labroye in 1984. We can see the wooded enclosure. The oval pasture marks the court of the old castle and the pit in the middle is covered by bushes.

Surrounded by wide moats which perhaps date from antiquity, Labroye means 'fortified place' in the Gaul language; the small château of Labroye was 'neither of great strength nor of great value', according to Monstrelet.

Labroye was burned in 1436 by British captain Thomas Kyriel.

We can only see on the drawing of 1560 (A) two towers connected by simple roofed buildings. Labroye was probably built of chalk and was totally destroyed by frost and later by exploitation of the ruins.

On the aquarelle by Montigny (B), Crécy lies to the left, the Authie flows in the background and the castle on its height comprises a watchman's tower that seems to have been added to the original drawing. We can see that the countryside has scarcely changed until very recent times.

According to Louandre, the castle of Labroye was owned in 1346 by Jean Lessopier, named Grand camp. It was he who opened the gates of the castle to the king of France 'not without the terrible tears and lamentations of all his subjects'.

'Fighting well, strong and unhurt.'

'Well,' replied Edward III, 'return. Tell him this is the time to win his spurs, and not to come looking for me whilst he is capable of holding his sword. If it is God and St George's wish, the day will belong to him!'

Nevertheless, faced with this French threat, Edward brought up the two battalions of Arundel and the prince. Edward was optimistic. From the windmill, that he would not leave, he could see everything. 'From there he could see the French position, which was so bad that it could not be worse! As they advanced, and engaged in battle, they threw themselves in recklessly and were lost.'

The battle of Crécy consisted, in total, of a clumsily linked succession of irregular charges. Even the contemporaries do not recall exactly how many there were. Ferdinand Lot says there were about fifteen or sixteen, all horribly bloody, becoming more and more laborious and slow, due to the difficult terrain, under an increasingly dark sky.

When it was obvious that the battle was going badly, the Moisne of Basle, who was still to be found in the king's entourage, said, heartbroken, 'My advice was not heeded. We have proceeded to lose everything.'

Jean de Luxembourg, the blind king of Bohemia, heard him and asked, 'What time is it, Moisne, and how is the enemy deployed?'

'Sire, it is very late and we have the sun full in our faces. Our lines are badly drawn and our men are falling under the arrows to no avail. It started like this: and it is impossible to change anything.'

The king of Bohemia then decided on the only possible end that befitted both his loyalty and his French links.

'Noble lords,' he said in his darkness, 'I beg you dearly, and by the faith that you owe me, to lead me into the fray of the battle so that I may die from the blow of a sword.'

'Willingly, my lord,' they replied simply. They tied the reins, hoisted a banner and raised the lances, and, on the orders of Moisne, six or seven knights and several squires launched an attack by themselves, Jean de Luxembourg in their midst. On the following day, their bodies were found among the carcasses of horses, their reins still tied together. The death of this blind man will be remembered for many centuries to come. Two equerries, Lambequin du Pé and Pierre d'Auvillers, escaped death and returned to tell of this suicide pact.

Behind the knights, a charge of footsoldiers was attempted. Thousands upon thousands of men-at-arms and freemen tried to approach the English, to fight hand-to-hand where the French could prove their worth. Edward, from his vantage point, watched them and he let them come, running and shouting; when he saw that they were within reach he gave the command to fire the arrows. The charge collapsed and withdrew in disorder. The English were impregnable.

Night began to fall. A motionless mass was strewn over the ground of Vallée-des-Clercs — Philippe de Valois' army.

No writer directly mentions the pikemen, but they had been at work. The number of dead and the lack of prisoners confirm this. Between the charges, when they were no longer endangered by arrows, the Welsh pikemen left the English ranks and went about their horrible business, indifferent to any plea. They went to slaughter without running any risk, from body to body peeling off the armour. Behind them nothing

'And they all replied, Willingly, my lord.'
Froissart, CCXXV.

78

THE CHAPEL OF THREE
HUNDRED BODIES

*An isolated chapel surrounded by green hedges
exists in the countryside between the villages of
Brailly and Maison-Ponthieu, at 10 km from
the English positions at Crécy. It is surrounded
by tombs of which none are more than 100
years old. This is the chapel of 'three hundred
bodies'. Tradition says that three hundred dead
French soldiers of the battle of 1346 were
buried there. On account of the distance this is
only plausible if they did not die during the
battle on the 26th but were killed on the 27th
during the massacre of the 'commoners'.*

*The Chapelle des Moriamini, between
Brailly and Gapennes, today follows the same
tradition according to Praron, but it is today
entirely ruined and the stone cross of
Millencourt is said also to have marked tombs
of the French who died in 1346.*

*Traditions can never be relied upon and
some people wonder whether the names of the
chapels are not due to simple verbal distortion.
The chapel of Trois Cents Corps is said to
have been the old chapel of Trochencourt, and
the chapel of Moriamini the old chapel of
Norio Mesnil which was cited before the
battle. Similarly, the cross of Jean de Bohème
might have been only a parish boundary cross.*

stirred, or hardly anything, for some must obviously have been overlooked. Night fell amidst the silence.

Louandre states that the Germans, who were serving in the English army, were amazed that no prisoners were taken. This was neither customary nor in the interests of the army.

'Sire,' they are reported to have said, 'we are very surprised that you support this spilling of noble blood. You could obtain large ransoms that would finance part of the war.'

The king told them not to be astonished, as 'he had issued instructions to kill everybody and it was better that it was such'.

He did not, therefore, take one prisoner.

There were also murmurings in the English ranks on seeing the Welsh slaughter. According to Jean le Bel, Edward III had to 'sound the trumpet and order that no one should pursue the enemy, nor loot, nor move the dead until they were authorised to do so in order that in the morning they could be recognised'.

'He also ordered that each soldier should go to his position and rest without laying down arms and that all nobles should come and dine with him.' Edward celebrated his victory whilst remaining wary. He knew that one danger remained, that of the crowd of free men and other contingents who still followed the French army.

The English therefore camped in their battle positions, tending large fires to light up the area and warn them of any nocturnal attack.

Night had fallen, and the battle was over.

Following the repeated advice of Jean de Hainaut and Charles de Montmorency, who remained at the king's side throughout, Philippe VI left when he

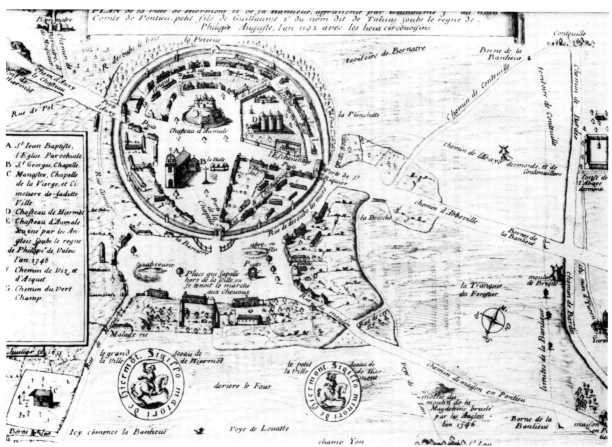

understood that he could expect nothing from this badly started battle. For a moment he had thought of emulating Jean de Bohème, but his marshals pointed out to him that this would be madness. Hainaut, Montmorency, Beaujeu, Saint-Venant, d'Aubigny, five knights and forty-two mounted men-at-arms were the king's only escort when, in the blackness of night, he left the site to the English, admitting defeat.★

The reason that he rode towards the north-east, to the castle of Labroye, six kilometres away, was because it was the nearest French stronghold (Abbeville was twenty kilometres away). He arrived after about an hour, in almost total darkness, having crossed the Authie. At Labroye, a small castle standing on a very wide and deep moat, the drawbridge was raised and the portcullis lowered.

The horsemen called up, and replies came from the ramparts. At Labroye they already knew that the day had been disastrous, as they had seen the wounded and deserters. No doubt they had also seen the lone figure of Thierry de Sancelles. Sancelles, a vassal of Jean de Hainaut, was riding a beautiful black horse that the king of France had presented that very morning to his master, whose banner he was carrying. During a charge, by a miracle, Thierry had cut through the English ranks, probably between the two battles, and found himself all alone behind the enemy. 'Not considering himself talented enough to return,' Froissart says kindly, he set off alone towards Doullens, in the direction of Arras, passing by Labroye. He arrived at Cambrai with Hainaut's banner.

From the rampart of Labroye they shouted, 'Who goes there?'

According to one source, no doubt true, but which seems legendary because it has been recounted so many times, the horseman replied from the outer edge of the moat, 'Open up, lord of the castle, it is the unfortunate king of France!'

They opened the gates in tears. Philippe and his escort were welcomed, took refreshment and soon left. Philippe rode on through the night, following the Chaussée Brunehaut, the old Roman way leading to Amiens. Before noon on the following day, the king of France had crossed the Somme, stopping at l'Abbaye du Gard, having covered nearly forty kilometres since Labroye. Philippe VI had been in the saddle for about thirty hours: this 53-year-old man had covered almost seventy kilometres since mass the previous morning at Saint-Etienne.

Sunday, 27 August 1346. A thick fog covered the battlefield. 'There was so much mist that one could

HIERMONT

The present village of Hiermont at 12 km from Crécy was in the twelfth century a built-up area of importance for the time; it had been given its liberty as a commune in 1192 and joined Amiens, Abbeville and Saint Riquier which alone had been granted this right until then. According to Louandre, Hiermont was defended by a wall with towers, built behind a circular moat which may have been very old; there were fourteen roads inside the walls and fifteen outside, and an hôtel de ville, markets, a big church and a little hospice. The Château d'Aumale lies in the centre built on a little hill by Jean de Ponthieu, Count of Aumal, towards the end of the twelfth century.

According to the history of the Count of Ponthieu, published in 1657, Hiermont was destroyed by the English in 1346, probably on the 27th of August, the day after their victory, when they plundered the countryside to a distance of 20 km from the battlefield. Hiermont, according to Louandre, is said to have been destroyed during the peasant uprising of 1358. It was again destroyed during the Spanish invasion of 1636. Seen from the air, this village still shows signs of its dramatic past.

★ Some people have written that the king himself was wounded, but this is unlikely, since he did not dismount until the end of the morning of the following day.

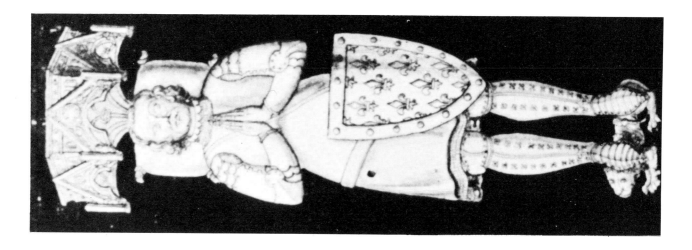

The only known likeness of a knight who died at Crécy, that of Charles d'Alençon, lay in the church of the Jacobins in the Rue Saint-Jacques in Paris, until the revolution. It was broken up in 1792, like so many others, but an engraving had been made between 1695 and 1715 by Louis Bourdan, at the request of the medievalist Roger de Gaignières (1642–1715). Charles d'Alençon, brother of King Philippe VI, was wearing armour that was modern for the time with a hauberk covered by a tunic down to the knees and characteristic of the middle of the fourteenth century. With hinged shoulder and elbow plates and hinged brassards, the first components of metal armour, called 'white harness', appeared on the scene. The leg armour seemed to be in painted or studded leather. The prince is depicted standing with no helmet.

★ It is always pointless to rewrite history, but one cannot ignore this astonishing fact: if Philippe de Valois, as advised by the Moisne of Basle, had waited until the following morning to attack, the English archers would not have been able to fire in the mist. In a side-arms battle it seems certain that the French would have won.

hardly see an acre of land.' The English, staying in groups around their fires that paled in the dawn, had not moved. They knew they had won, and they knew they had suffered very few losses; but it was not yet over. The French army was numerous and it was still possible that, beyond the mist, that army was regrouping. Edward, to whom the archers were of no use in fog, redeployed them as plain footsoldiers. He sent 500 men-at-arms and 2,000 archers to reconnoitre the enemy, if any were left. ★

There were, effectively, some left, in particular the militia of Rouen, Amiens and Beauvais, 'who had slept in the thickets, ditches and hedges and were asking each other where they were, what had happened to them, and where their king and lords were', according to Jean le Bel.

When they saw the English coming towards them through the fog, walking casually as if on a stroll, they waited for them because they thought that they were their own people. 'The English penetrated into their midst as wolves amongst sheep and killed them at will.'

The English killed about 8,000, says Froissart, who liked large numbers. If there had not been a mist he insists that there would have been many more.

All day long the English scoured the countryside. In the fog they came by surprise across troops from Rouen, who were searching for Philippe's army under the orders of the Lord of Amposte, a knight recently returned from Rhodes where he had fought the Turks. All were killed. Elsewhere, others escaped: 500 lances from Savoie were to reach Montreuil behind the backs of the English.

According to an ancient annal of Abbeville, the *Goddons* advanced on the town, in order to attack it, from the opposite side to the side chosen for their previous attack on the 23rd, 'but it had such good defences that they retraced their steps burning everything in their path'.

There were no further French troops around Crécy. The damage could now be assessed.

That morning, having attended mass, Edward summoned Cobham, whom he asked to return to the scene of the battle, accompanied by knights conversant with coats-of-arms and all heraldry, and 5,000 men. Their task was to return the bodies, count the corpses, list the names of knights who could be identified and put the princes and nobility aside so that a service could be said according to their rank.

Louandre maintains that an old tradition, preserved in the Abbaye de Valloire, says that Edward gave the order to look for any wounded and to give them assistance. It is said that the Cistercian monks of Valloire rescued a large number of barons and soldiers and carried them to their estate at Crécy-Grange, about a kilometre to the north of the windmill, where they administered treatment. 'There is still an enclosure,' Louandre says, 'the place where these disciples of Saint-Bernard prepared a burial-place for the valiant knights that they had not been able to save.'

All day long, Cobham and his men drew up their macabre inventory. On the battlefield they met French who, like them, were looking for specific bodies amongst this massive charnel-house. They helped each other politely. The task was so enormous that Cobham and his men did not return before nightfall. When Cobham finally submitted the figures to the king, Edward realised the extent of his triumphal success. Cobham had found eleven princes, a prelate, 80 standard-bearing knights, 1,200 knights and 15–16,000 equerries, commoners, Genoese and foot-soldiers. The English losses (one hesitates to accept them) consisted of only three knights and fifteen archers. Jean le Bel, probably more accurate, says they amounted to 300. In any event they were very slight.★

The French losses were so heavy, it was said in France, that for 200 years never had so many princes been killed in a single battle, not even at Bénévent or Courtrai. The whole of France and every noble family was affected. Besides Jean de Luxembourg there were also, among the most important, Charles Count of Alençon, the king's brother, Louis of Châtillon Count of Blois, the Duke of Lorraine, Jean de Châlons, Louis de Sancerre, Jean d'Auxerre, Louis de Nevers Count of Flanders, the Count of Aumale, the Bishop of Sens, the Archbishop of Nîmes, Jean de Croï, Lord of Airaines, the Counts of Salm and Blamont, the Count of Harcourt and his sons. Of particular note was the loss of Jean d'Harcourt, one of Geoffroy's brothers,

★ Lord Byron said that he had lost two ancestors at Crécy, Paul and Hubert Byron, but nothing is more suspect than family tradition!

whose war cry 'Harcourt, Harcourt' was heard as he died.

On Sunday, Jean's body had been identified by Geoffroy. Louandre says that his helmet had a peacock's tail intertwined with gold as its crest. Geoffroy, who was now a disgraced vassal, banished knight and his brother's murderer, later (with the noose around his neck) threw himself at his king's feet, and Philippe pardoned him.

On Monday 28th, the clearing up began.

That morning, heralds from the French army came to negotiate a truce of four days to bury the dead. The truce was signed.

Edward, in mourning, attended a funeral service with his son, surrounded by all his officers. Jean le Bel confirms that afterwards he left Crécy, having first taken the bodies of the English killed to 'the abbey in the forest on the edge of the woods, so that they received a decent burial and God's blessing'.[1]

The English army set off again towards the north, and camped that evening on the banks of the Authie, again pillaging and burning. The following day, the 29th, the army arrived at Montreuil. However, the Count of Savoie and his brother, the Count of Geneva, together with 500 lances, were defending the ramparts of the town, having arrived too late to fight at Crécy. Edward III burnt down the outskirts and went on his way. He set fire to Etaples, Waben and Saint-Josse, plundered the region around Boulogne and decided to besiege Calais. This was his first siege since 12 July, scarcely fifty days earlier, when he had landed at Saint-Vaast-la-Hougue. Now, however, he had re-established communications with England and it would appear that he had received cannon: the town was to fall eleven months later.

At Crécy the inhabitants of the town and those of the neighbouring villages had been summoned to bury the dead. It was a gruesome task, but also, perhaps, a windfall: there were clothes, armour, iron, carts, horses and — maybe — money and certainly medals.

Firstly the corpses were stripped. Armour, clothes and weapons were given to the English, who shared them amongst themselves. However, so much was left after the English had chosen what they wanted that they made a big pile of armour and weapons, mixed in with carts, and burnt the lot: burnt iron was of no use.

Thousands of unidentified corpses were thrown into communal ditches. In 1844 Louandre wrote, 'one can still see these large ditches into which the soldiers were thrown'. One of these ditches can be found where the valley meets that of La Maye.[2]

1. The English dead were possibly buried in the cemetery of the Forest l'Abbaye (eight kilometres), effectively on the edge of the wood but on the other side of the forest of Crécy: or possibly at Maintenay. Maintenay, however, like Valloire, is more than nineteen kilometres away.

2. Today it is a store for building materials. Aerial surveys have revealed nothing of these ditches.

Edward III of England leaving his tent, at the start of the siege of Calais. The date is theoretically September 1346 and the English camp was to become a true town from which the tents disappeared within a short time. The king is wearing a hat covered by a light crown. To receive a messenger dressed in civilian clothes, he is wearing a cloth jacket with a lace collar placed directly on his armour. Note his beard and long hair. The marshals around him are entirely dressed in armour, an anachronism because this did not yet exist in 1346. On the frieze around the tent, we can read an astonishing sign written in French, 'Vive Edouard'! There is no wording on the other tents, also made of rich embroidered cloth. Four bombards can be seen on the right firing on Calais. These heavy guns which must have weighed several hundred kilograms are fixed on static mountings. A very simple device allows them to be aimed in height but not in direction with each gun on a wooden cradle mounted on ball joints that swivel on the mounting. Each gun must have been carried in the form of several loads on carts. They probably came from Dover to join the English army in front of Calais, rather than having followed the army marching through the north of France, without firing a shot.

Traces of depressions. The recent reallocation of land has caused the disappearance, between Crécy and Wadicourt, of the boundaries between fields. Photographs taken recently from the air, in December 1984, reveal a number of wide depressions which may be ancient farm ponds which have disappeared, or some of them may be a burial pit for forces killed in 1346, like that at the bottom along the old track. The place name of Le Marché à Charognes ('the place of dead horses'), appears to substantiate this idea. Other depressions were visible in 1840, says Louandre, at the point where the Vallée des Clercs meets the vallée de La Maye.

The other is against a small gully on the slope of the hill which was held by the English.

At the top of the Vallée-des-Clercs there is the gloomy place called 'Le Marché à Charognes'. Carcasses of men (and also perhaps horses) were no doubt amassed here.

The most important bodies were taken away, some remains being taken to the abbeys of Maintenay and Valloire, but most to the church of Crécy. It is here that the Count of Flanders was buried. The body of the Count of Alençon was sent to Amiens. Philippe VI only learnt the full extent of the disaster on Tuesday morning with the return of the heralds and knights despatched to Edward of England to negotiate the truce.

Philippe expressed his grief at having lost this flower of nobility, dying in vain but without hesitation. He read the list of the hundreds and hundreds of dead. His army had been crushed, his relations killed and his friends slain. This king, who had lost — ten to one — the battle against Edward, was now surrounded by those whom death had spared and who had managed to rejoin him.

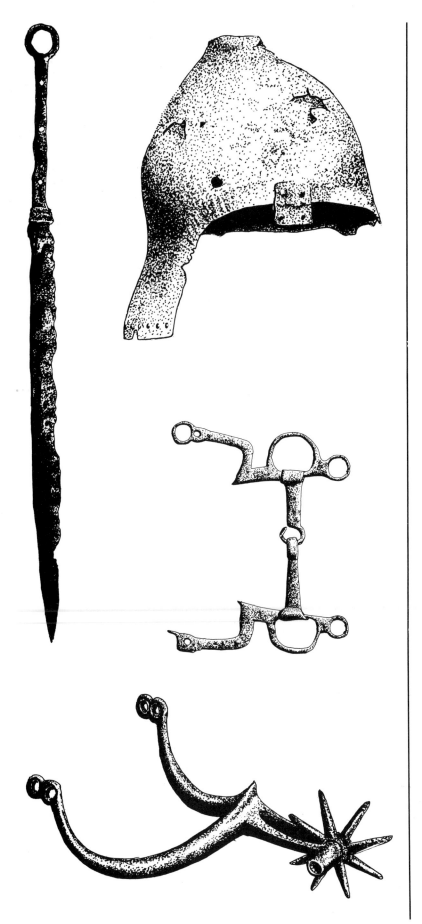

a. A basinet found in the Authie region, at Ponches-Estruval, about 8 km to the north of Crécy. This basinet, which was perhaps contemporaneous with the battle, was modified later, the re-cut cheeks in particular, with a hinge riveted above. We can see the lacing holes by which the tunic was attached to it.

b. A dagger 37 cm long, made in one piece of beaten iron that was originally fitted with a handle in wood or horn. Same origin as the basinet.

c. Fourteenth-century bit, now in the Musée de l' Armée.

d. The spurs supposed to have been found at Crécy, and to have been offered to the Musée de l' Armée by Boucher de Perthes in the nineteenth century. It is surprising that the celebrated pre-historian did not keep this remarkable item in his own museum at Abbeville.

For a while the king looked for a scapegoat for the disaster and wanted to hang Godemars du Fay. Had du Fay not let the English escape to the north of the Somme? 'But did the whole army do any better at Crécy?' Philippe was asked. The king admitted it had not. Godemars was pardoned and became Sénéchal de Beaucaire.

Philippe left 'le Gard' after a few days. Having attended a funeral service at Amiens, he arrived at the Abbey of Moncel on the edge of the forest of Halatte, where he became a recluse.

In Paris, and throughout Europe, Crécy was to make an astounding impression. The French court had

Edit. Dagheau

Built after the battle, broken, and then restored with care during the nineteenth century by Dr Boucher, of Fontaine, the cross of Jean de Bohème was mounted on a base in 1906 with the unsuccessful intention of enhancing its appearance. It is shown here as it stood originally under the tall trees of the chemin-de-l'armée. The trees have disappeared, as has the track, but this cross remains as the only authentic monument to the battle of 1346.

It is not very probable that this monument marks the place where King Jean died with his squires from Bohemia, Henri de Rosemberg and Jean de Leucstemberg, because it is at a distance of more than three times the maximum range of the English bows. According to Louandre, who gives details of his sources, it is more probable that King Jean, when grievously wounded, was picked up by the English. 'Edward was told that he was still breathing and ordered that he should be spared and carried to the king's tent', where he died. Out of the rich clothing of the German sovereign, the English king only kept the ostrich plumes tied with golden braid above the helmet and the German motto Ich dien ('I serve') engraved on it. Edward gave it to his son as an award for his exploits of the previous day. Succeeding Princes of Wales have kept the motto and the plumes in their coat of arms.

The body of King Jean was then placed in the chapel of the Abbey of Valloire where the following inscription could still be seen during the eighteenth century: 'Jean Luxembourg, king of Bohemia, was brought and placed here in the year one thousand fourteen hundred and sixty-three'. Louandre says that the coats of arms of fifty knights who died with him on the same day were placed around his tomb. This contradicts Froissart who says that Jean was buried at Maintenay, 2 km away.

'Carried into the cathedral of Luxembourg, desecrated during the revolution, placed among the curiosities of a potter near to Treves, the remains of Jean de Boheme are today (1844) in the palace of the King of Prussia on the banks of the Saar...'

A photograph exists of the last 'Edward's mill' at the location of the present underground water reservoir of Crécy, but it is not illustrated in this book — this mill built of white stone could not have been built before the seventeenth century and it was knocked down in 1898.

been the most ostentatious and Philippe the most powerful sovereign in Europe. The first Valois king, who could not save Calais, was soon to finish his reign in humiliation. The parliament of 1347 would confirm his dishonour, and he would die four years later. His son John (who had criticised his father's behaviour) fought in the battle, when he found himself face to face with the English at Poitiers, and was taken prisoner.

In 1346 the triumphant Edward III created, in St George's church at Windsor, the Order of the Garter, to reward those of his officers who had served him best at Crécy. 'Garter' was the Welsh word used on the day of the battle for 'rallying'.

According to Henry Martin, Crécy was 'an historic event...the cavalry beaten by the infantry, the feudals beaten by their incurable lack of discipline, the excessive weight of their equipment and harness...an automaton virtually unable to move apart from in a straight line'.

Today, in our eyes, Crécy is primarily the victory of the objective over the legendary, discipline over goodwill, efficiency over heroism, and ability over passion.

Crécy should, in theory, have signified the end of feudal armies.

THE FRENCH LOSSES ACCORDING TO THE DIFFERENT SOURCES

Froissart (*Man. d'Amiens*)	11 princes, 2 prelates, 1,285 knights, 15–16,000 footsoldiers
M. of Northburgh (eye-witness)	1,542 dead (not counting the footsoldiers)
Villani	1,600 knights, more than 4,000 mounted squires: 20,000 dead in total
Louandre quoting *Histoire de Dauphiné*	1,716 princes and knights, and about 10,000 footsoldiers
F. Lot	Uses Froissart's figures, except for the footsoldiers: 30,000
E. Lavisse	3,800
C. Rothero	4,000

DID CANNONS FIRE AT CRÉCY?

There are a number of indications, but no proof. The first written work that speaks of cannon fire is the story of an Italian, Villani, who was alive at the time of the battle but was in prison in Florence. 'The fire of the bombards made so much noise that it seemed that God himself was thundering!'

Jean le Bel does not speak of any cannons and neither did Froissart when he first wrote his Chronicles. He only speaks of bombards in the second version of his document, after Villani's statement. There is therefore nothing very convincing on the French side of the Channel.

The English writers of the time do not speak of artillery. Yet Hereford B. George wrote in the Battles of English History in 1895, 'there is no intrinsic impossibility of Edward III possessing cannons at Crécy'. He continues, 'They were present immediately afterwards at the siege of Calais, although they were of very little use'. Joseph Hunter quotes texts dated 1344 and 1347 proving that Edward III already possessed cannons that were fired with powder in London at the time.

According to the historical secretary of Woolwich Artillery Museum, there is no knowledge in England of any cannon that was supposed to have been used at Crécy. The first cannons had no wheels and were carried on carts. Could they really have followed the track from Saint-Vaast to Crécy and never fired a shot? Did Edward III, who took great care in selecting his expeditionary forces, encumber himself with heavy guns and never fire a shot? This can definitely be doubted because he avoided any form of siege or direct assault.

A number of cannon balls have been found on the site, the first in 1850 which was in cast iron and of diameter 24 cm. It was 'heavily damaged by rust'. It was put on display in a café of Abbeville and disappeared in the fire of 1940. Four other iron cannon balls, all of the same diameter — 8.4 cm — placed behind the cross of Jean de Bohème were removed by a collector. Three of them are at present displayed with horseshoes and a stirrup at Crécy with the following wording 'probable vestiges of the battle of Crécy, dug up when prospecting the chemin de l'armée at the end of the eighteenth century. Offered by the family Desjardin.'

These cannon balls are all in cast iron but we know that cast iron cannon balls only appeared during the reign of Louis XI. No proof can therefore be given by material facts.

Whatever the truth may be, the action of these bombards, if any, had no impact on the battle. But the echo of the hypothetical cannon shot fired by Villani continues to roll through time; if true, it would have been the first cannon fired during a land battle in history.

Louandre is certain about the cannon, while Favier and Vasseur speak without taking up any position. Ferdinand Lot expresses frank doubts.

BIBLIOGRAPHY

Numerous historians have studied this battle, amongst them Jean le Bel and Froissart, the Flemish Gilles de Muisit, the Italian Villani and the English Henry Knigton. They all agree on the basic facts.

Froissart began the writing of his chronicle in 1361. He is sometimes accused of being pro-English, having lived across the Channel. A second draft revised by Froissart, which is less biased towards England, and is known as the *Manuscrit d'Amiens*, appeared in 1376. It is known that Froissart was nine years old at the time of the battle of Crécy, that he used as his sources Jean le Bel (1290–1370), the canon of Liège, who was serious and restrained and, later on, Villani (1276–1348) who is the subject of more controversy. (The author worked from the Droz edition of Froissart, Geneva 1972, by George T. Diller, edition of the Manuscript of Rome, late 869.)

The general background to this book was gathered from reading authors of this era, in particular Ernest Lavisse, Ferdinand Lot and Jean Favier.

L'histoire d'Abbeville et du comté de Ponthieu ('The history of Abbeville and the County of Ponthieu'), by F.-C. Louandre, Abbeville-Paris, 1844, then 1883, proved a varied and accurate source. Louandre worked from local archives and in particular *L'histoire des mayeurs d'Abbeville* ('The history of the mayors of Abbeville'). He visited the sites, noted the traditions and verified the texts at the locations. The majority of quotes are assigned in the text.

Finally, the author used various publications from the *Bulletin de la Société d'Emulation Historique et Littéraire d'Abbeville*, notably 1902, 1906 and 1943, as well as the *Notes pour servir à l'histoire d'Airaines* by the Abbé Marchand, Abbeville, 1909.

Picture Credits

Photographic cover, pp. 14 and 15, Bibliothèque Nationale, Paris, Cabinet des Manuscrits; p. 13 Bibliothèque Albert 1er, Brussels; p. 16 I.G.N. Map by Cassini (coloured) 1750; p. 23 Breslau Manuscript, Berlin, Battle of Kadzand, negative Giraudon; p. 25 B.N. Paris, Cabinet des Estampes, Coll. Gaignières; pp. 28 ph. Rivet; p. 31 ph. Emile Bourgey; p. 32, 72, 80 I.G.N. Paris; pp. 35, 40, 45, 71, 77, 79, 86 author's collection; p. 39 Rivet de Mont Devie map, Coll. D. de Saint Amand, detail of the Cordier map, Bibliothèque Municipale of Abbeville, Cl. Giraud; pp. 35, 36 and 45 ph. Roger Agache; p. 47 ph. Servas; p. 48 Dominique Burgat; pp. 62 and 63 ph. Musée du Bargello, Florence (inv. R 272); pp. 64, 66, 67, 69a, b and c Cl. Giraudon; p. 69 ph. du Musée de l'Armée, Paris; p. 80 III from the l'Histoire généalogique des comtes de Ponthieu R.P. Ignace de Jesus Maria, Paris 1657, Bibliothèque Municipale d'Abbeville, Cl. Giraud; p. 76 Regional Archives, Amiens J. 789 and Gouache d'Adrien de Montigny, Bibliothèque Clementine, Prague (Vol. XXIII/A9, scene 99a), Courtesy of Gerard Bacquet; p. 82 Bodleian Library, Oxford (Coll. Gaignieres), Courtesy of Christopher Rothero; p. 85 Chronicles of England (Jean de Warin, 15th century, B.N. Paris, Cabinet des Manuscrits, 87 Fo. l), Cl. Giraudon; p. 88 ph. CLB.

Illustrations:
Pp. 35, 36, 43, 52–53, 59a and b, 60c and d, 61e and f, 70, 71, 73, 87a, b, c and d author's collection; pp. 56–57 Robert Lescaux.

ACKNOWLEDGEMENTS

The author would like to thank all those who were willing to give him access to sources and share their knowledge of texts, iconography, terrain, horses, weapons and, in particular, archery: Madame Agache-Lecat, Curator of the Abbeville Library; Monsieur François d'Anzel d'Aumont, Président de la Société d'Emulation d'Abbeville; Monsieur Jacques Liepens, Directeur de Haras; Monsieur Reverseau, Curator of weapons of the *haute époque* at the *Musée de l'Armée*; Monsieur Bernard de Senneville, Member of *l'Arc Club de France*.

The publishers of this edition would like to express their thanks to Christopher Rothero for his advice and to Abdus and Joanna Sookia for their diligent translation for the French.

INDEX

References in *italic* refer to illustrations.